THE STUDY OF LITERATURE AND RELIGION

The Study of Literature and Religion

An Introduction

David Jasper
*Director, Centre for the Study of
Literature and Theology, University of Durham*

Fortress Press   Minneapolis

Cover illustration: *The Sun* by Edvard Munch (reproduced by
permission of Munch Museet: Oslo Kommunes Kunstsamlinger).

Library of Congress Cataloging-in-Publication Data
Jasper, David.
The study of literature and religion/David Jasper
p.   cm.
Bibliography: p.
1. Christianity and literature.   I. Title.
PN49.J39 1989   809'993382—dc 19   88–29998
ISBN 0–8006–2325–8

3573J88 Printed in Hong Kong 1–2325

For Ann Loades
Teacher and Friend

Contents

Preface

As an introductory volume to the interdisciplinary study of literature and religion, this book makes no claim to completeness. Each
chapter may be regarded as a particular exercise in a relationship
which seems to me to be almost inexhaustibly fertile, and my
purpose is not to argue for any single critical position. I have
deliberately restricted my concerns almost entirely to a discussion
of the Western and Christian tradition, and my purpose is to begin
to explore in very preliminary ways some of the issues which will
be dealt with in much greater detail in subsequent volumes in the
series. If this book does nothing more than persuade a few readers
of the importance of the reading of literature for theology, and,
conversely, of the inescapably religious end towards which the
study of great works of the imagination points us, then I shall be
content.

My claims to originality in the particulars of my discussions are
limited. Friends and colleagues will be quick to recognise the
fruits of numerous conversations, and I readily acknowledge my
indebtedness to the ideas and insights of many of them. In
particular I thank Margarita Stocker, F. W. Dillistone, John
Coulson, Robert Detweiler, Lynn Poland and J. R. Watson. Joanna
Denver valiantly created a typescript from my original manuscript.
Most of all I thank my wife Alison and young daughter Hannah
for their patience and their sense of fun. Taking oneself too seriously is a great danger for any critic or theologian.

An earlier version of Chapter 3 first appeared in *Theology* in
March 1986, published by SPCK; part of Chapter 7 appeared in
Literature and Theology in March 1987, published by Oxford University Press. I am grateful to both these publishers for allowing me
freedom to use this material.

The author and publishers wish to thank Faber and Faber Ltd and
Oxford University Press Inc, who have kindly given permission

to reproduce the poem 'The Annunciation' from *The Collected Poems of Edwin Muir* (1964), copyright 1960 by Willa Muir.

Durham   DAVID JASPER

If words are not THINGS, they are LIVING POWERS,
by which the things of most importance to mankind
are actuated, combined, and humanized.

S. T. Coleridge

1

Introduction

I

This book has been writing itself for a number of years. As is so often the case, it exists to correct, or at least revisit, some of the claims of my earlier books. An author never quite means what he says or says what he means, and so must try again. And yet the confusions remain and even grow. What I have to say, therefore, is not finished or complete. It is, rather, a series of explorations into various ways in which literature and theology interact with one another, each having in common the assumption that theology is of ultimate and irreducible importance.

That assumption needs to be made and clearly stated. For, on the one hand, the industry in 'religion and literature' which has been growing, particularly in the United States, since the 1950s, seems to take as its starting point various assumptions about *literature* and to presume a creative and intellectual supremacy in professional literary criticism and literary practice. Instead of living dangerously within a creative dialectic – literature and theology – the industry has tended to claim competence in an odd new discipline, 'literature and religion', with an apparent desire (sometimes stated as a clear objective, as in David Hesla's recent essay 'Religion and Literature: The Second Stage') to abandon theological categories and study religion as a phenomenon within culture, sociological, anthropological, even psychological. The programme is, in the words of Professor Giles Gunn, 'to reconstitute the discussion on the plane of the hermeneutical rather than the apologetic, the anthropological rather than theological, the broadly humanistic rather than the narrowly doctrinal'.[1] The list is an odd one, and simply will not do. The tendency is to banish the entire theological enterprise (and here I limit myself to the Judaeo-Christian tradition), its philosophy, spirituality and sense of the finite and infinite, to vague terms like 'otherness' and

1

'alterity'. Religion (and literature) without commitment. It is simply incorrect to claim, as Theodore Ziolkowski does in his book *Fictional Transfigurations of Jesus*, that contemporary writers are even capable of transcribing the pattern of the New Testament story 'with the detachment of the non-believer who sees the story with wholly neutral eyes'.[2] Upon such neutrality scriptural literature will make its judgement.

On the other hand, and the second point leads on from the first, much twentieth century literary theory seems to take its origins from a theological anxiety. In his book *Literary Theory* (1983), Terry Eagleton attributes the growth of English studies in the later nineteenth century to 'the failure of religion' (p.22). But if the churches were, for various reasons, failing to reach Victorian hearts and minds, the religious questions remained and surface repeatedly and curiously in some of the most apparently secular and deconstructive of modern critics. In his introduction to the collection entitled *Deconstruction in Context*, Mark C. Taylor writes:

> From its beginning, Western philosophy points towards the constructive subject that is always remaking the world in its own image. As such, philosophy transforms theology into anthropology. The implications of ontotheology become explicit in Hegel's identification of man with God. By attempting to deconstruct both the constructive subject and the horrifying world it has created, Derrida points beyond the certainty of absolute knowledge to the uncertainty of postmodernity. Always arriving late, forever coming second, and never returning on time, deconstruction repeatedly demonstrates the impossibility of modernity by soliciting the other which, though never present, 'always already' haunts presence. As the end of modernity, deconstruction is postmodern; Derrida is the postmodern whose letters bear a message that never arrives.[3]

Those words haunt me, for theology – albeit theology transformed – lies at their root. We shall find ourselves returning repeatedly to Jacques Derrida and to 'deconstruction' in the pages of this book, because I perceive in Derrida an honesty and a refusal to surrender to objectivity which does bear fruit in a truthfulness and which reminds me of Coleridge's warning: 'He, who begins by loving Christianity better than Truth, will proceed by loving his own Sect or Church better than Christianity, and end in loving himself better than all' (*Aids to Reflection*, 1825).

Thus loving ourselves we remake the world in our own image. But in Kierkegaard in the nineteenth century, and in the later Wittgenstein, Merleau-Ponty, Derrida and others in our own, the search for objective certainty in self or metaphysical system is replaced by open-endedness, an objective uncertainty both bold and passionate. The deepest concerns of theology are conceptually abandoned and revisited, as the Marxist Maurice Merleau-Ponty put it, 'we have to reformulate the sceptical arguments outside of every ontological preconception and reformulate them precisely so as to know what world-being, thing-being, imaginary being, and conscious being are'.[4] I am, of course, aware that I am extending my reading of these deconstructionist critics in ways of which they would hardly approve. But no doubt they would recognize the freedom of a text to take us (as opposed to *them*) whither it will. As Derrida writes in *Margins of Philosophy* (1982), we must abandon nostalgia, 'a lost native country of thought,' and yet affirm with play, 'a certain laughter and a certain step of the dance. From the vantage of this laughter and this dance, from the vantage of this affirmation foreign to all dialectics, the other side of nostalgia, what I will call Heideggarian *hope*, comes into question'.[5]

Some of the chapters which follow will endeavour to establish a proper context for these preliminary thoughts. What I am suggesting here is, first, that a rediscovery of theology is essential to contemporary reflections on philosophy, literature and culture, and that second, theology must be prepared to be reinvigorated by these radical reflections. As David Jenkins expressed it years ago:

> The dreadful thing about so much theology is that, in relation to the reality of the human situation, it is so superficial. Theological categories (really mere theological formulae) are 'aimed' without sufficient depth of understanding at life insensitively misunderstood. Theologians need therefore to stand *under* the judgements of the insights of literature before they can speak with true theological force of, and to, the world this literature reflects and illuminates.[6]

II

This book it may be said, continually moves between two approaches – the radical and philosophical looking at linguistics since Saussure and straying into deconstruction, and the more traditional and strictly 'literary'. With the former we walk closely with that startling statement in a sermon of Eckhart, 'Man's last and highest parting occurs when, for God's sake, he takes leave of God', a remark now familiar through the writings of Don Cupitt, with all their incisiveness and limitations. It is balanced, therefore, with the latter, and here the focus will be initially upon the figure of T. S. Eliot and his crucially important essay of 1935, 'Religion and Literature'.

In the middle years of our century the development of the New Criticism in literary circles in the United States of America owed not a little to the essays of Eliot, who remarked of literary criticism that 'there is no method except to be very intelligent'. The principles of New Criticism (a branch of Formalism or what is generally, and rather vaguely, described as Structuralism) can be simply stated. The critic is required to abandon all 'extraneous' material – the biography of the author, historical context – and formulate criticism from within the 'sealed and sovereign' context of the work. Literature is to be regarded as autonomous, a self-sufficient structure not directly linked with any 'real' world outside. Form and content are regarded as inseparable, the structures and literary devices of a work being creative of meaning (see further below, pp. 87ff and 98ff)

Critics have seen the early stages of Religion and Literature, at Chicago and Drew Universities in the 1950s, as a theological reaction against the sealed autonomy of New Criticism. Theologians set out to disprove this autonomy and to assert the 'theological meanings and dimensions' of poetry.[7]

This may have been so, but it was nevertheless true that almost all the proponents of 'religion and literature' studies in America, and particularly those engaged in literary approaches to the Bible, have been children of the New Criticism or, in various ways, structuralists.[8] As will be seen in this book, the insights of formalism have proved to be extremely stimulating despite their limitations. And it is precisely these limitations, perceived most acutely by Paul Ricoeur, which have tended to steer the whole enterprise away from theology towards an essentially trivial notion of 'religion', a phenomenon to be observed dispassionately from literary standards claiming to be the arbiters of what constitutes true knowledge.

Yet the extravagant claims of literature may be seen to be less reprehensible when it is recognized how, during the last hundred years or so, religion has gradually withdrawn from the literary and artistic context of Western culture, and the theologian has become increasingly 'un-lettered' if not illiterate. In the words of John Coulson:

> His subject matter, no longer taken for granted culturally, is not thought to be fitted for general study as part of a liberal education. Instead, he has laboured in seminary confinement, and become the prisoner of his theological explanations, which are sharply defined, unmysterious, and rigid.[9]

I recognize my purpose as a revisitation of theology, returning to it through literature and recovering something of those uncomfortable, sometimes even unwelcome qualities of a lack of definition, of mystery and fluidity.

The danger, however, is the arrogance of literature in the context of what is confessedly and ultimately a theological and religious concern. Take, for example, these lines from Yeat's poem 'Wisdom', in which the 'true faith' seems to be a contrivance of the artist and poet.

> The truth faith discovered was
> When painted panel, statuary
> Glass-mosaic, window-glass,
> Amended what was told awry
> By some peasant gospeller;
> Swept the sawdust from the floor
> Of that working-carpenter.
> Miracle had its playtime where
> In damask clothed and on a seat
> Chryselephantine, cedar-boarded,
> His majestic Mother sat
> Stitching at a purple hoarded
> That He might be nobly breeched
> In starry towers of Babylon
> Noah's freshet never reached.

The artist in this poem is one whose craft and creative genius corrects and builds upon the crudities of the 'peasant gospeller' (St. Mark, perhaps?), and in his artifice discovers the true faith. Here is literary art exalting itself and its crafted inspiration above the primary revelation and literary evidence (not so naïve after all) of the apostolic age.

Yeats's burnished poem in no way reflects the spirit of this essay. For we shall be living in risk-laden, untidy and even disordered territory, avoiding the pursuit of any clear methodology. We shall be concerned with the challenge and even conflict which literature and theology present to one another, with what Arthur Koestler called the collision of matrices, and Paul Ricoeur the conflict of interpretations.[10] Certainly the early and ambiguous relationship of the formal study of Religion and Literature with American New Criticism has had unfortunate consequences. First, the focus of attention has remained firmly upon the business of *literary* evaluation, seen now in terms of ethical and very occasionally theological considerations. Second, it has the tendency to promote the false assumption that all literature is religious, which, as Ziolkowski points out, is 'a different matter altogether from insisting that all literature may be viewed from a religious-ethical point of view'.[11] And still prime consideration is being given to literature. And if, as we have seen David Jenkins point out, theology needs to stand under the judgements of the insights of literature, it is equally true that poetry needs religion and the theologians, even poetry which is subversive of religion. This is discussed at length in Chapter 2, 'Poetry, Belief and Devotion'.

But the subservience of theology to literature as a critical stance has a history which goes back beyond the nineteenth century. It is a part of a process of secularization which exalts the poet and artist as a kind of priest of the imagination, a modern prophet replacing ancient prophecy and its inspired utterance. The notion of the poet as prophet was deeply embedded in English and German Romanticism,[12] while at the end of the nineteenth century the prolific but now almost forgotten critic and Broad Churchman, Stopford Brooke (1832–1916) insisted that poets are natural theologians in whose minds originates the theology which theologians spoil by their intellectual endeavours. In poets 'we see theology, as it were, in the rough; as, at its beginnings'.[13] Poets have a prophetic role, and that in the most religious sense, 'to bid men look forward and labour for not only their own country's highest good, but for the restoration of all things, to keep the hope and faith of a millenium ever before our eyes, to be the Prophet of mankind, (p.229).

For Brooke, at the end of a tradition of Romanticism, the poetic imagination has claimed the role of the theologian. Often, too, and not least among the Victorians, literature has been used as merely a tool for religious propaganda, sugaring the pill of dry dogma and doctrinal proposition. It is against such a broad background that T. S. Eliot's 1935 essay 'Religion and Literature' seems so important and distinguished.

Eliot states his case quite clearly in his opening paragraph.

Literary criticism should be completed by criticism from a definite ethical and theological standpoint. In so far as in any age there is common agreement on ethical and theological matters, so far can literary criticism be substantive. In ages like our own, in which there is no such common agreement, it is the more necessary for Christian readers to scrutinize their reading, especially of works of imagination, with explicit ethical and theological standards. The 'greatness' of literature cannot be determined solely by literary standards; though we must remember that whether it is literature or not can be determined only by literary standards.[14]

In the first instance, it seems, literature and literary criticism requires the supplement of theology and ethics for its completion. Nor is this simply 'religious literature', but all literature. One might indeed go further and suggest that religion is the senior party, to the standards of which literature is merely a supplement; literature judged merely on its proximity to the Christian faith. But then, in his final sentence, Eliot asserts the determinative power of 'literary standards', so that literature remains, in a sense, something complete in itself with literary criticism a powerful tool. An ambiguity is thus expressed – literature *and* religion, independent and yet inextricably involved with each other. For literature requires the assessment of ethical theological standards which operate only in conditions already defined by literary standards.

Here is a paradox indeed! For while it implies the independence of the two categories involved, it also denies it. Thus, while literary standards may define the Authorized Version of the Bible as 'great literature', Eliot would castigate the people who enjoy it *solely* because of its literary merit as essentially parasites (pp.389–90). Its influences is more complex than that, for

> the Bible has had a *literary* influence upon English literature *not* because it has been considered as literature, but because it has been considered as the report of the Word of God. And the fact that men of letters now discuss it as 'literature' probably indicates the *end* of its 'literary' influence.
>
> (p.390)

There is, according to Eliot, a department of literature which might be described as 'religious', writing which may be theologically and ethically pure yet with no more than minor significance as literature. Such literature fails to treat 'the whole subject matter of poetry in a religious spirit', omits the 'major passions' and confesses its ignorance of them. Among such 'minor' writers, Eliot instances Vaughan, Southwell, Crashaw, Herbert[15] and Hopkins. We may or may not agree with his judgements but at least we should recognize his endeavour to free the consideration of 'literature and religion' from the limitations of devotional or even religious propagandist elements, however worthy these may be. He asserts quite plainly: 'I am concerned with what should be the relation between Religion and all Literature' (p.391).

In his essay, Eliot proposes a paradoxical and uneasy relationship between these two substantive categories. Each retain their independence, yet each both judge and require the other. It is a relationship both unstable and fertile, uncertain and living, contingent and yet organized. It is, above all, vitally necessary. For literature rescues religion from the dangers of dogmatism, blunt apologetic and crudely direct evangelism. While religion provides necessary ethical and theological standards to remind literature of the dangers of a beauty which serves evil or destructive ends. Nor is the play of this paradox upset by Eliot's recognition that underlying the relationship is the fundamental and final mystery of divine revelation translated into the language of scripture and expressed in the Christian tradition. If this seems to some people like making religion the privileged partner of the hierarchy, then it can only be said that it makes the paradox more profound, the relationship likened to the incarnational mystery in which is met the human (the literary) and the divine (the religious) in a united yet distinct partnership.[16]

Much of this book deals with contemporary literary theory, literature and theology. This, and its untidiness, is a reflection of my own experience of intellectual and indeed spiritual struggle in an area with precious few rules or established landmarks. Many of my concerns are, of course, as old as literature or theology themselves, an essentially metaphysical preoccupation forever suffering disproval. If most, though not all, of my energies are expended upon worrying over the implications of Saussurian linguistics, hermeneutics and Paul Ricoeur, and Derridan postmodernism, that is not to deny that the Western literary progression (some might say regression) from 'words' to 'the Word' must recognize, the literary, religious and linguistic implications of Plato, Aristotle, Philo, Eusebius, Thomas Aquinas, Sidney, Leibniz, Coleridge, Shelley – indeed, almost everybody in the Western tradition.

What follows, then, is a personal reflection which is intended to promote further discussion and to raise questions. It represents a series of staging posts on the way, and no doubt will need to be rewritten as discussion develops. If some parts offend, others, I hope, will indicate my concerns for Christian devotion and spirituality – that this is not simply an exercise in brutal intellectualism. Perhaps, in the end, I have been guided more than anything else by a sentence of Eliot in 'Religion and Literature'.

It is not enough to understand what we ought to be, unless we know what we are; and we do not understand what we are, unless we know what we ought to be. The two forms of self-consciousness, knowing what we are and what we ought to be, must go together.

(p.399)

2

Poetry, Belief and Devotion

At breakfast on Friday, 11 June 1784, Dr Johnson informed Boswell that he did 'not approve of figurative expressions in addressing the Supreme Being'.[1] Beginning with Johnson's complaint in the *Life of Waller*, that religious poetry is actually an impertinence, this chapter will consider four states of the relationship between Christian belief and poetry. The second state will be represented by poems of Yeats and Kipling, neither of whom have claimed to be Christian believers in any orthodox sense. Each, however, drew deeply upon Christian association, and found in the traditions of Christianity a tremendous resource for their poetry. The third state concerns three ostensibly Christian writers, the poets George Herbert, W. H. Auden and Edwin Muir, whose poetry reflects their sense of religious commitment and whose vision of religious truth inspires their poetry. Finally, I shall consider that often under-estimated form of poetry which John Wesley described as 'the handmaid of Piety', the congregational hymn.

The second part of the chapter will examine more theoretically questions of the nature of religious poetry, the definition of Christian verse, and the relationship between the task of the poet and the work of the theologian. I shall conclude by giving some attention to a modern theologian who was peculiarly sensitive to the power and insights of poetic writing – Austin Farrer.

I

1. A distaste for religious poetry is by no means restricted to those who may count themselves irreligious. Dr. Samuel Johnson was a pious man, and, wrote Boswell, presented 'his dissertation upon the unfitness of poetry for the aweful subjects of our holy

religion. . . . with uncommon force and reasoning'.[2] (Boswell, it should be said, admitted that he could not agree with Johnson on this point). The Doctor's most sustained attack on 'poetical devotion' is in his *Life of Waller*.

Let no pious ear be offended if I advance, in opposition to many authorities, that poetical devotion cannot often please. The doctrines of religion may indeed be defended in a didactick poem; and he who was the happy power of arguing in verse, will not lose it because his subject is sacred. A poet may describe the beauty and the grandeur of Nature, the flowers of the Spring, and the harvests of Autumn, the vicissitudes of the Tides, and the revolutions of the Sky, and praise the Maker for his words in lines which no reader shall lay aside. The subject of the disputation is not piety, but the motives to piety; that of the description is not God, but the works of God.

Contemplative piety, or the intercourse between God and the human soul, cannot be poetical. Man admitted to implore the Mercy of his Creator, and plead the merits of his Redeemer, is already in a higher state than poetry can confer.

The essence of poetry is invention . . .

From poetry the reader justly expects, and from good poetry always obtains, the enlargement of his comprehension and elevation of his fancy; but this is rarely to be hoped by Christians from metrical devotion. Whatever is great, desirable or tremendous, is comprised in the name of the Supreme Being. Omnipotence cannot be exalted; Infinity cannot be amplified; Perfection cannot be improved . . .

Of sentiments purely religious, it will be found that the most simple expression is the most sublime. Poetry loses its lustre and its power, because it is applied to the decoration of something more excellent than itself. All that pious verse can do is to help the memory, and delight the ear, and for these purposes it may be very useful; but it supplies nothing to the mind. The ideas of Christian Theology are too simple for eloquence, too sacred for fiction, and too majestick for ornament; to recommend them by tropes and figures, is to magnify by a concave mirror the sidereal hemisphere.[3]

On his dismissal of 'contemplative piety' as a proper subject for poetical attention, and his admission of a place for didactic poetry, and poetry in praise of the creation in religious discourse, Johnson may commend himself to the rigid dogmatist, either Christian or atheist.[4] For the defence of the doctrines of religion in didactic verse restricts poetry to a theological task of edification concerning a state of grace which is clearly to be identified from the rest of secular experience. It is a state which either dogmatist will readily identify, and accept or reject. Poetry in praise of the creation is safely at one remove from religious danger, concerned not with God himself but with the works of God. Again, therefore, the rigid Christian may find it a useful defence and support: a dogmatic atheist will understand its subject and his own reasonings for rejecting it.

But the heart of religion which is 'the intercourse between God and the human soul', is, according to Johnson, matter too high for poetry. For if the purpose of poetry is to enlarge our understanding and fire our imagination, then it must fall far short in treating of a Supreme Being whose perfection is infinite and beyond further improvement. Poetry here is simply out of its depth, and Johnson concludes his remarks by a further rejection of 'tropes and figures', the use of figurative language in religious poetry. This disapproval of figurative expressions, not only in religious poetry, but in all religious language reveals a restriction in Johnson which is the product of what Coleridge was later to describe in *The Statesman's Manual* (1816) as 'an unenlivened generalizing Understanding'. Coleridge was actually speaking of the 'mechanic philosophy' of the tradition of John Locke (1632–1704), but more generally, his criticism could be directed towards any dreary theology of edification and plain reasonableness which denies to religious discourse the creative exercise of the imagination.

Lord David Cecil in his Introduction to *The Oxford Book of Christian Verse* (1940) shares Johnson's distaste for religious poetry, but for rather different reasons, and based upon a different theory of poetry. They agree about the feebleness of most religious poetry, and that, in Cecil's words, 'the very loftiness of the religious sentiment is in part responsible' (p.xi) But if for Johnson 'sentiments purely religious' have a sublimity, a power and a purity which place them beyond the reach of poetic art, for Cecil, it is because 'pious emotion' is, in most people so fleeting and feeble that 'the faintness of their experience reflects itself in the verses in which they seek to communicate it'. For exactly opposite reasons it seems religious poetry is poor and unnatural. According to Johnson, the poet simply cannot reach the heights of divine truth. For David Cecil, Christian doctrine and orthodoxy prevent the poet's 'spontaneous expression of the spirit' (p.xxi), 'with the consequence that much Christian verse is, by an aesthetic standard, insincere' (p.xiii).

2. In his Introduction to *The New Oxford Book of Christian Verse* (1981) Donald Davie writes that 'W. B. Yeats is one example that springs to mind of a poet who is without doubt a greatly religious poet, who is no less clearly a non-Christian poet, the member of a church whose doctrine – though glancingly divulged by fragments in Yeats's poetry and prose – has yet to be formulated' (p.xx). It is nevertheless true that Yeats drew deeply upon the Christian tradition in much of his verse. Was it simply that he found in its images, rites and dogmas a great poetic resource, yet one among many? In his own words in 1937.

When I was young we talked much of tradition, and those emotional young men, Francis Thompson, Lionel Johnson, John Gray, found it in Christianity. But now that *The Golden Bough* has made Christianity look modern and fragmentary we study Confucius with Ezra Pound, or like T. S. Eliot find in Christianity a convenient symbolism for some older or new thought . . .[5]

Did his new understanding of the continuity of myth, learnt from his reading of Frazer's *The Golden Bough* simply prove to him the fragmentariness of Christianity, a religion with images significant yet indeterminate? The poet's address to the Creator in the last two stanzas of 'A Prayer For My Son' expresses Christian doctrine with precision rather than indeterminacy.

> Though You can fashion everything
> From nothing every day, and teach
> The morning stars to sing,
> You have lacked articulate speech
> To tell Your simplest want, and known,
> Wailing upon a woman's knee,
> All of that worst ignominy
> Of flesh and bone;

> And when through all the town there ran
> The servants of Your enemy,
> A woman and a man,
> Unless the Holy Writings lie,
> Hurried through the smooth and rough
> And through the fertile and waste,
> Protecting, till the danger past
> With human love.

Here, most precisely, are the great images of the Christian doctrine of the Incarnation: the creator of all things emptying himself and in humility revealing himself in human shape (Philippians 2.6–8). As vulnerable flesh, he makes himself dependent on human love for protection during the massacre by Herod's soldiers of the children of Bethlehem (Matthew 2:16). The prayer of the father for his son is express in perfectly orthodox Christian terms. The doctrine is, of course, made contemporary and personal, as the father pleads that the Incarnation may be powerfully and lovingly present in the sickness of his child.[6]

In 'A Prayer For My Son', the prayer is genuine and the Christian doctrine is quite clearly expressed. Yet equally, Christianity was by no means the only resource for Yeats' poetry. He was well-read in Vedic literature, had studied Buddhism, Rosicrucianism, and the myths of Greece. Each, it seems, represented for him something important and fundamentally human. Nevertheless, the range of Yeats's religious reference, and his lack of personal commitment to a specific Christian belief, need not prevent us from describing 'A Prayer For My Son' as a Christian poem. The Christian faith and Christian symbolism, it seems, retained a special power for Yeats even though he would not call himself a Christian. He may not commend himself to the rigid dogmatist, who may have understood well Dr Johnson's clear distinction between the sacred and secular, but to the reader who is not sure where the secular ends and the sacred begins, who is not sure of the limits and definition of the Christian or even the religious element in human life, and for whom a religious tradition speaks not through dogma but through what is most deeply felt and experienced in human life.

Rudyard Kipling is certainly a minor poet beside Yeats, although it is said that in Edwardian England there were houses where the only books known were Kipling and the Bible. He was a life-long agnostic with a profound sense of the transcendent and an eclecticism as broad, though perhaps less well-informed, as that of Yeats. He wrote in a letter: 'I expect that every man has to work out his creed according to his own wave-length, and the hope is that the Great Receiving Station is tuned to take *all* wave-lengths.' In later life he was profoundly aware of 'something incomprehensible but certainly not chance. . . . a Mercy at which man can only look over his shoulder occasionally, sometimes in terrified awe, sometimes in an almost affectionate mockery'.[7]

Much of Kipling's verse draws upon biblical associations and the Christian tradition. His early poem about Anglo-Indian life, 'The Story of Uriah', is prefaced by words from Nathan's parable to David. 'Now there were two men in one city; the one rich and the other poor' (2 Samuel 12:1). A much later poem, 'The Prodigal Son (Western Version),' places the familiar parable in the contemporary context of a rich younger son sent overseas alone and without guidance who finds life safer and more acceptable among the pigs for 'there's no reproach among swine, d'you see,/For being a bit of a swine'. In such poems, Kipling's use of the Bible is simply employing what is culturally familiar without any religious commitment or vision.

Certainly Kipling, despite his aversian to the orthodoxy of a 'cold Christ and tangled Trinities', appreciated the faithful performances of Christian duties and service.

> Eddi, priest of St. Wilfrid,
>   In his chapel at Manhood End,
> Ordered a midnight service
>   For such as cared to attend.
>
> But the Saxons were keeping Christmas,
>   And the night was stormy as well.
> Nobody came to service,
>   Though Eddi rang the bell. . . .
>
> And when the Saxons mocked him,
>   Said Eddi of Manhood End,
> 'I dare not shut His chapel
>   On such as care to attend'.

But if the virtues celebrated in this poem hardly make for good poetry, Kipling finds inspiration when poetry draws upon Christian doctrine as it enters and illuminates the mysteries of the human situation. 'The Rabbi's Song' from *Actions and Reactions* (1909), begins with the potentialities for good and evil of human thought, and moves towards a meditation upon the Christian theme of redemptive suffering.

> If thought can reach to Heaven,
>   On Heaven let it dwell,
> For fear thy thought be given
>   Like power to reach to Hell.
> For fear the desolation
>   And darkness of thy mind
> Perplex an habitation
>   Which thou hast left behind . . .
>
> Our lives, our fears, as water,
>   Are spilled upon the ground;
> God giveth no man quarter,
>   Yet God a means hath found,
> Though Faith and Hope have vanished,
>   And even Love grows dim-
> A means whereby His banished
>   Be not expelled from Him.

The key word is 'means'. The poem is subtitled '2 Samuel xiv 14', which reads: 'We needs must die, and are as water spilt upon the ground, which cannot be gathered up again; neither doth God respect any person; yet doth he devise means that his banished be not expelled from him.'

The reference is Old Testament, the 'singer' of the poem is a Jewish rabbi, the poet an agnostic, and yet here is a fine and precise statement of the Christian doctrine of redemption, powerful even though the human faculties of faith, hope and love grow dim. Like Yeats's 'A Prayer for My Son', Kipling's 'The Rabbi's Son' draws profoundly and personally upon a central Christian mystery.

Clearly doctrine and symbolism remain powerful for Yeats and Kipling, not least, perhaps, because they are so deeply embedded in the culture in which they lived. Their poetry required this particular element if it was to plumb the depths of the human

society which was its concern; for it remains a profoundly forma-
tive element in our society, even if it is one which we may choose
to challenge, reject or ignore. But also, in Yeats and Kipling,
religion and poetry require one another. For poetry may be
tempted to assume some of the functions of religion, and in doing
so it risks restricting its own freedom, moving towards fixity and
a particularity of commitment which will harden its imaginative
texture and limit its range. On the other hand, as we have seen
in Yeats and Kipling, it is not the indeterminacy but the precision
and definition of theology and the language of belief which
provides for poetry a means of exploration. The point is very
similar to the one made by T. S. Eliot in 'Religion and Literature,'
and Eliot again proposes a similar relationship between religion
and humanism – clearly distinguished yet each requiring the other
– in his essay 'The Humanism of Irving Babbitt' (1928). The task
of humanism (or indeed poetry) is not to provide dogma, but to
refresh and correct the petrifying tendencies of religion which
must strive, nevertheless, to attain a clear identity and definition.
Eliot writes:

> Any religion of course is for ever in danger of petrifaction into
> mere ritual and habit, though ritual and habit be essential to
> religion. It is only renewed and refreshed by an awakening of
> feeling and fresh devotion, or by the critical reason. The latter
> may be the part of the humanist. But if so, then the function of
> humanism, though necessary, is secondary. You cannot make
> humanism itself into a religion.[8]

3. If the humanist, then, renews religion by the critical reason, the
poet, perhaps, refreshes it by an awakening of feeling. Unlike
Yeats or Kipling, George Herbert (1593–1633) was a devout Christian who never wavered in his resolution to devote his poetic
gifts to the service of God. Yeats and Kipling certainly employed
Christian doctrine in their poetic reflection upon human life.
Herbert lived the doctrine, and the concrete and particular images
of his poetry authentically ground his belief in the world in which
he lived. If, for Yeats, Christianity was in the end no more than
'a convenient symbolism for some older or new thought', for
Herbert it was a matter of commitment. In the words of R.S.
Thomas, 'it was the commitment to an order of reason, discipline

and propriety, embodied in a church solidly based on Scripture and the Book of Common Prayer'.[9]

Herbert did not therefore write didactic verse of such as Dr Johnson might have approved. His commitment to Christian belief entailed a particular morality and order of life, and though this discipline the beauty of the world was perceived. His very saintliness made him deeply conscious of sin and of the finitude of worldly beauty, yet the world was beautiful for him, nevertheless.

> Sweet day, so cool, so calm, so bright,
> The bridall of the earth and skie:
> the dew shall weep thy fall tonight;
> For thou must die.

('Vertue')

Nor were the arts neglected as instruments for praise and devotion. Herbert was a fine musician, and a musical sensitivity directs some of his most beautiful and polished verse.

> Come, my Joy, my Love, my Heart,
> Such a Joy as none can move:
> Such a Love, as none can part:
> Such a Heart, as joyes in love.

('The Call')

He was fortunate, too, to live at a time when the English language was fresh and vital, and he knew it.

> Let forrain nations of their language boast,
> What fine varietie each tongue affords:
> I like our language, as our men and coast:
> Who cannot dress it well, want wit not words.

('The Sonne')

Not only was Herbert's vocabulary drawn extensively from the Book of Common Prayer and the worship of the Anglican church. His poetry meditates finely upon Christian doctrine – in 'Love' upon the sacrament of Holy Communion.

Love bade me welcome: yet my soul drew back,
    Guiltie of dust and sinne.
But quick-ey'd Love, observing me grow slack
    From my first entrance in,
Drew nearer to me, sweetly questioning
    If I lack'd anything.

Certainly Herbert is recommending the idea of God in figurative
language – as a host; the Host? Omnipotence cannot be exalted,
Dr Johnson maintained, and perfection cannot be improved. But
who can say that the poem, and indeed the sacrament itself, does
not 'enlarge our comprehension' of a mystery which lies beyond
our reasonable understanding? The poetry does not claim perfection or omnipotence, but God's very uniqueness and infinity
demand the language of metaphor and riddling allusion by which
poetry may lead to an intensification, a transfiguration even, of
our imperfect apprehension of what is perfect.[10]

Herbert's poem is not addressed to God, nor is even about God
directly. Such poetry would indeed be an impertinence. It is rather
a reflection upon a secular, human situation concerning the laws
of hospitality and relationship, and an invitation to think about
these virtues of forgiveness and kindness as if they were perfected.
The poem is entirely human, and yet disturbing, for no human
host could ever be so perfectly courteous and gentle. The numinous and transcendent has become disturbingly immanent.

For Dr Johnson poetry is talkative but knows its limitations. In
Herbert, poet and believer (and belief is primary), the words weave
images in patterns that end in silence. He would have agreed with
A. M. Allchin in the recognition that the primacy of silence,

> prevents us from falling into the fatal error of thinking that
> we have comprehended and can express the fulness of God's
> revelation whether in a closed system of human concepts or
> in purely human and worldly artistic techniques. . . . Like the
> monastic community, like the whole church, the work of an
> artist or a theologian (then) becomes an eschatalogical sign of
> the presence in this age of the indescribable glory of the age to
> come.[11]

The verbal precision required for poetry to lead us to a silence that
is unique to Christian belief, is found in Herbert's poem 'Prayer'.

Prayer the Churches banquet, Angels age,
    Gods breath in man returning to his birth,
    The soul in paraphrase, heart in pilgrimage,
The Christian plummet sounding heav'n and earth;

Engine against th' Almightie, sinners towre,
    Reversed thunder, Christ-side piercing spear,
    The six-daies – world transposing in an houre,
A kinde of tune, which all things heare and fear;

Softnesse, and peace, and joy, and love, and blisse,
    Exalted Manna, gladnesse of the best,
    Heaven in ordinarie, man well drest,
The milkie may, the bird of Paradise,
    Church-bels beyond the starres heard, the souls bloud,
    The land of spices; something understood.

The poem is a series of images which require considerable intellectual application, and reflect very precisely upon Christian doctrine and scriptural reference. The second stanza meditates upon Atonement and Judgement. The third stanza softens into a series of evocative images, biblical, and domestic. Finally, by allusion and in figurative language, we are brought to the point where the mysterious 'something' which is prayer, is yet known in the intense experience of the poem. Words have brought us closer to the silence of perfection.

I conclude with briefer references to two modern Christian poets, Edwin Muir and W. H. Auden. Edwin Muir's poem 'The Annunciation' describes quite simply and pictorially St. Luke's account of the visit of the angel Gabriel to Mary. The language never attempts theological discourse or explanation. It is almost purely descriptive, and, again, its stillness and quietness lead us to the edge of a silence held between 'the ordinary day' and eternity. In the intensity of the meeting, the mystery of the Incarnation is, quite literally, conceived.

The angel and the girl are met.
Earth was the only meeting place.
For the embodied never yet
Travelled beyond the shore of space.
The eternal spirits in freedom go.

See, they have come together, see,
While the destroying minutes flow,
Each reflects the other's face
Till heaven in hers and earth in his
Shine steady there. He's come to her
From far beyond the farthest star,
Feathered through time. Immediacy
Of strangest strangeness is the bliss
That from their limbs all movement takes.
Yet the increasing rapture brings
So great a wonder that it makes
Each feather tremble on his wings.

Outside the window footsteps fall
Into the ordinary day
And with the sun along the wall
Pursue their unreturning way.
Sound's perpetual roundabout
Rolls its numbered octaves out
And hoarsely grinds its battered tune.

But through the endless afternoon
These neither speak nor movement make,
But stare into their deepening trance
As if their grace would never break.

In Muir's poem the images are precise, as precise as the commitment to the significance of the meeting between Gabriel and Mary; but through the accepted mystery of faith we are led into an intense and silent reflection which is beyond words or definition.

W. H. Auden's Oratorio *For the Time Being* (1944) is also an extended poetic meditation on the Annunciation, the Nativity and the mystery of the Incarnation. In the section 'At the Manger' Mary sings a lullaby to the infant Jesus, modern in its self-consciousness, and, in Helen Gardner's words, it 'could not have been written before the mid-twentieth century. It is post-Freud in conception, post-Eliot in rhythm and vocabulary'.[12]

Sleep. What have you learned from the womb that bore you
But an anxiety your Father cannot feel?
Sleep. What will the flesh that I gave do for you,

Or my mother love, but tempt you from His will?
Why was I chosen to teach His Son to weep?
Little One, sleep.

Dream. In human dreams earth ascends to Heaven
Where no one need pray nor ever feel alone.
In your first few hours of life here, O have you
Chosen already what death must be your own?
How soon will you start on the Sorrowful Way?
Dream while you may.[13]

Again, Auden is deeply committed to the Christian mystery of the God made Man, and in Mary's lullaby, as in Yeats's 'A Prayer for my Son', the doctrine is given a contemporary and even personal focus. The universal nature of poetry written under such inspirations is recognized by Auden when he wrote:

> The impulse to create a work of art is felt when, in certain persons, the passive awe provoked by sacred beings or events is transformed into a desire to express that awe in a rite of worship or homage, and to be fit homage, this rite (which in poetry is verbal) must be beautiful. This rite has no magical or idolatrous intention; nothing is expected in return. *Nor is it, in a Christian sense, 'an act of devotion'*.[14] (my italics)

Auden was a professing Christian, Yeats was not. Yet it would be difficult to define Auden's lullaby as 'Christian' and 'A Prayer for my Son' as 'Non-Christian'. Such distinctions would be dangerously exclusivist, and would judge the poetry simply by what we know, or imagine we know, of the poet – a fallacy of intention. In the end, however, the task of poetry is the imaginative one of looking hard at what is the case and sharpening our perceptions of the truths about humanity. In this task it will often be seen to conform with the great truths of religion which lie at the very centre of our being. But the Christian, and the Christian poet, will go further, for he is committed, in a way that poetry is not, to a vision and to a story by which all other things are lived and defined. That, finally, is why we must make a distinction between Yeats and Auden or Herbert.

4. Dr Johnson, we may imagine, would not altogether have disapproved of John Wesley's preface to the *Collection of Hymns for*

the Use of the People called Methodists (1780). Wesley was clear about
the subordinate role of poetry, and a proper didacticism in hymns
intended to teach and confirm doctrine.

> That which is of infinitely more moment than the spirit of
> poetry, is the spirit of piety . . . I would recommend [this collec-
> tion] to every truly pious Reader, as a means of raising or
> quickening the spirit of devotion, of confirming his faith; of
> enlivening his hope; and of kindling and increasing his love to
> God and man. When Poetry thus keeps its place, as the hand-
> maid of Piety, it shall attain, not a poor perishable wreath, but
> a crown that fadeth not away.[15]

Johnson, however, was dismissive of the verses of Isaac Watts
(1674–1748), one of the finest of eighteenth century Protestant
hymn writers,[16] and no doubt would have concurred with Lord
David Cecil in his statement that 'the average hymn is a by-word
for forced feeble sentiment, flat conventional expression' (op.cit.,
p.xi).

At worst, this is certainly true. But there are many fine hymns
whose very limitations are often a strength, and which remain for
many people genuine expressions of joy and sorrow, hope and
despair. They should not, therefore, be despised. Watts himself,
the author of such familiar hymns as 'O God, our help in ages past'
and 'Jesus shall reign where'er the sun', wrote of the necessary
restraints which are laid upon the hymn writer.

> In many of these composures, I have just permitted my verse
> to rise above a flat and indolent style; yet I hope it is everywhere
> supported above the just contempt of the critics: though I am
> sensible that I have often subdued it below their esteem; because
> I would neither indulge any bold metaphors, nor admit of hard
> words, nor tempt the ignorant worshipper to sing without his
> understanding.[17]

Hymns are verses with a specific task to do. They have to be sung,
and to be immediately comprehensible to a congregation. They are
an adjunct to worship and not solitary reflections upon religious
experience. They are concerned with Christianity in its public
form, as *doctrine*. At best, therefore, they are vehicles for a fine,
sharp intellectualism, using compressed and clear language to

express the concrete and particular matter of Christian belief. (We may recall how Yeats and Kipling found that the precision and definition of theology and the language of belief provided for poetry a means of exploring the depths of humanity.) From the pen of Isaac Watts;

> Hosanna to the royal son
>   Of David's ancient line!
> His natures two, his person one,
>   Mysterious and divine.
>
> The root of David, here we find,
>   And offspring, are the same:
> Eternity and time are joined
>   In our Immanuel's name.

Poetry here is indeed the handmaid of piety, and of theology. But the best of Watts' hymns also have genuine aesthetic qualities, examples of a Calvinist art of simplicity, sobriety and measure. Their very limitations are their art, a deliberate frugality which is all the more aware of beauty in the truths of the religious belief which sustains the human soul.

In 'A Short Essay toward the Improvement of Psalmody', Watts asserted that 'it was hard to restrain my verse always within the bounds of my design; it was hard to sink every line to the level of a whole congregation, and yet to keep it above contempt'. In a way, this disciplined Calvinist aesthetic of sobriety is similar to the Tractarian doctrine of reserve as it is expressed in John Keble's hymns drawn from *The Christian Year* (1827), although its purpose is very different, indeed, almost opposite. For if Watts's restraint arose from an awareness of the limitations of his congregations, Keble's reserve was a means whereby strong passions are restored to tranquillity and wholeness under the formal structures of poetic form; an aesthetic doctrine of poetry as a cloak for inspiration.

But Keble's reserve, like Watts's restraint, made him a writer of enduring hymns; 'Blest are the pure in heart', 'There is a book, who runs may read', 'Sun of my soul, thou Saviour dear'. And as Johnson dismissed Watts as a poet, so Keble dismisses Johnson as a critic of religious poetry in his 1825 review of Josiah Conder's *The Star in the East; with other Poems* entitled 'Sacred Poetry'. Against Johnson's statement that 'the topics of devotion are few'.

Keble demands, 'How can the topics of devotion be few, when we are taught to make every part of life, every scene in nature, an occasion – in other words, a topic, of devotion?'[18] For Keble devotion encompassed all creation and all of human behaviour. He proceeds to defend the use of figurative language and the poetic exploration of the 'particulars' of the Divine perfection and omnipotence. The poet's task is to arrest the mind and, by limiting the scope of its contemplation, 'force or help her to think steadily on truths which she would hurry unprofitably over'. The poet is not a theologian, and his purpose is not to discuss and formulate theological doctrine. It is rather to commend doctrine and describe 'the effect of it upon the human mind'. For Keble, sacred poetry is not be identified with theology, for it has a quite specific task.

> . . . that one great business of sacred poetry, as of sacred music, is to quiet and sober the feelings of the penitent – to make his compunctions as much of 'a reasonable service' as possible.
>
> (p.176)

That was why Keble wrote such good hymns, appreciated by one so little attuned to the Christian faith as D. H. Lawrence.

> Sun of my soul, thou Saviour dear,
> It is not night if Thou be near –

> That was the last hymn at the board school. It did not mean to me any Christian dogma or any salvation. Just the words, 'Sun of my soul, thou Saviour dear,' penetrated me with wonder and the mystery of twilight.[19]

Lawrence continued to respond to such hymns long after he rejected the 'didacticism and sentimentalism' of religious teaching and the cant of 'Christian dogma'. Keble's hymn affected him with a sense of wonder and mystery; he loved the poetry with a *natural religious sense*, even while despising the Christian doctrine which it was written to serve.

Even in hymns, therefore, the art of poetry retains some autonomy, and the definition of 'Christian' in the idea of Christian verse is not easy. Yeats can write an apparently genuine and deeply moving 'Christian' prayer. Lawrence can love a John Keble hymn and yet deny vigorously any personal commitment to Christianity. Nevertheless a hymn as poetry must be limited by certain demands; in order to be sung it must be rhythmically stable; it must be readily understandable; its reference must be bound by orthodox belief.[20] Hymns are required to mean something, while a poem, we right say, *is* something, and means itself. The result is that hymns do not generally employ language suggesting a plurality of meanings or shifting perspectives. That is why the poetry and imagery of hymns can enter so profoundly and penetratingly into our senses, as Lawrence described it. It is to their theology rather than their poetry that hymns usually owe their burden of 'paradox and strange continuity'.[21] Charles Wesley's language in the following verse is deeply theological and Christological.

> O Love divine! what hast Thou done?
>   The immortal God hath died for me!
> The Father's co-eternal Son
>   Bore all my sins upon the tree;
> The immortal God for me hath died!
>   My Lord, my Love is crucified.

The hymn is based upon the theological conviction that Jesus Christ, the son of God has revealed himself and acted for me *sub contraria specie*, 'under the opposite kind'. The verse demonstrates the Christological principle of the *communicatio idiomatum*: that is, 'the transference of epithets appropriate to the human or the divine nature of Christ either to each or to the total unitary subject of the incarnation'.[22] The poetry of Wesley's hymn is perfectly straightforward for a congregation to sing and understand. Its doctrinal principles however go behind the poetry to the mysterious paradox before which language can only wonder and admit the primacy of silence.

In conclusion, it should be said that this delicate relationship between theology and poetry in the tradition of the hymn (and particularly the Nonconformist tradition) has resulted in at least one poet of the first rank, the American Emily Dickinson (1830–86). Living all her life in New England she was immersed in the tradition of Isaac Watts, Augustus Toplady and the Wesleys. All her poetry reflects the discipline, the simplicity, sobriety and measure, of the dissenting aesthetic. Within this tight poetic discipline Emily Dickinson appropriated her spiritual heritage and reshaped it into an idiosyncratic and deeply personal religious vision. Without discarding her belief in God she is able to sustain a profound emotional hold upon her sense of the Divine mystery within the stability of her verse (bound by it rather as Lawrence was emotionally bound by Keble's hymn). Resting upon this aesthetic discipline, Dickinson is able to work upon the perspective and paradoxes of her inherited Christian vocabulary, theology and doctrine in establishing her new vision outside the bounds of orthodoxy. The result in Emily Dickinson, however, was the transcending of the hymn form and the slipping of theological paradox into the multiple meanings, shifts and evasions of great poetry. Unlike hymns, her poems cease to mean anything, merely themselves.

> This was a Poet – It is That
> Distills amazing sense
> From ordinary Meanings –
> And Attar so immense
>
> From the familiar species
> That perished by the Door –
> We wonder it was not Ourselves
> Arrested it – before –
>
> (*The Complete Poems*, No.448)

II

1. In the first part of this chapter I looked at four ways in which religion and religious belief may be related to poetry. No attempt was made to draw any particular conclusions from this survey. It may be said generally, however, that the discussion throughout implied that there is a clear distinction to be made between religion or theology and poetry and that they are not to be confounded or made identical. In this second part of the chapter, some critical discussions of the nature of religious and Christian verse will be surveyed, concluding with a more theological look at the nature of 'poetic truth'.

Cardinal Newman in his early essay 'Poetry with reference to Aristotle's Poetics' (1829) affirmed his belief in the close connection

between 'the religious principle' and 'poetical feeling'. Hume and
Gibbon he believed, were radically unpoetical because they lacked
religious feeling. For Newman it was a plain fact that revealed
religion is essentially poetical.[23] All revealed truth is poetical, and,
Newman asserts, 'with Christians a poetical view of things is a
duty'. Indeed, to live a Christian life and to display the Christian
virtues of meekness, gentleness, compassion, contentment and
modesty, is to live the life of poetry. Equally, in all the great poets,
the source and condition of their poetry is religious virtue and
'right moral feeling'.

In his failure to draw any clear distinction between religion and
poetry, Newman ends up with a position in which 'poetic' means
little more than the good and morally correct. That which is bad,
debased or vicious is, by definition unpoetic, as is that which
wants 'religious principle'. Newman concludes accordingly that in
Dryden's *Alexander's Feast* 'there is something intrinsically
unpoetical in the end to which it is devoted, the praises of revel
and sensuality'. In the same way he would reject Byron's *Manfred*.
This particular conflating of the religious and the poetic is ultimately as sterile and insensitive as Dr Johnson's attack on 'poetical
devotion'.

Newman was a fine theologian, but a poor poet. Most editors
of modern collections of religious or Christian verse are literary
critics, and the invariable confusion which their writings and prefaces produce arise out of the fact that they fail to attribute a specific
or serious task to theology. Let us consider the opinions of the
editors of four books of religious poetry. Three of them, Helen
Gardner, Donald Davie and Peter Levi, begin by acknowledging
a problem of definition. Levi, the editor of the most recent of these
collections, *The Penguin Book of English Christian Verse* (1984), begins
his introduction:

> By the vaguest definition, Christian poetry might be any verse
> written by a Christian, or in a Christian framework or language,
> in Christian centuries, in a Christian society. By the narrowest,
> it might be whatever poem had a good angel for a muse, what-
> ever poem purely and deliberately expressed Christianity.
>
> (p.19)

But it is clear that Levi is unwilling to begin either to define
clearly what Christianity is, or to identify any culture or society

as Christian. Such unwillingness may be justified, but Christian theology nevertheless does provide doctrinal evidence of itself within universal human activity, as we have seen in the different cases of Yeats, Kipling and Herbert. Levi never addresses himself to poetry of the Incarnation, Redemption or the Resurrection. The particular doctrines of the Christian religion are replaced by a vague discussion of 'decent ways of talking about God'. This vagueness concerning religion and Christianity inevitably results in Levi's general failure to distinguish Christian poetry from any other kind of poetry. He writes:

> The faults and excesses of language that are unacceptable in religious poetry are unacceptable in all personal poetry. The problems of Christian style are only a part of the problem of all poetry.
>
> (p.23)

Certainly Levi wants to make a distinction between poetry and 'Christian activity' (though neither are given any definition). And it should be said that, although this lack of definition is a serious fault in his writing, Levi is fundamentally correct in refusing to identify a distinct category of Christian or even religious poetry. Poetry, as poetry, must be judged by universal criteria, and, its greatness established by literary standards, it may address itself to Christian theology or religious doctrine which perhaps may be illuminated by literary attention. Yeats or Herbert, therefore, may be capable of fine 'Christian' verse, because both are fine poets, and not because they may or may not be Christians.

This is also Donald Davie's position in *The New Oxford Book of Christian Verse* (1981). Davie shares with Levi a confusion born of theological poverty, although he does attempt to define what is specifically Christian in terms of a body of doctrine and a narrative of historical events (p.xxi). But he admits candidly that the concept, 'Christian verse', will not stand up to close scrutiny. He rejects Lord David Cecil's earlier distinction between sacred and secular verse, and abides by uncompromising standards of *artistry* in making, his selection (p.xviii). He despises religiosity and 'yeasty yearnings towards "the transcendent" '.

However, attractive and intelligent Davie's introduction may be, its weakness is evidenced by the fact that most of it is devoted to a discussion of the plain aesthetic virtues of the Nonconformist poets and hymn-writers – William Cowper, Isaac Watts and Charles Wesley – whom he finds particularly attractive. He is making a literary judgement concerning the 'sort of language . . . most appropriate when I would speak of, or to, my God'. (p.xxix). The limitations of this judgement, which would avoid any sort of prevarication or ambiguity as unseemly, arise from the apparent failure by Davie to recognize the creative power of Christian theology and the enormous and complex possibilities of exploring the nature of faith and belief when that power meets the expressive energies of words in poetry.

The Introductions to two further books of religious poetry can be dealt with more simply. Lord David Cecil in *The Oxford Book of Christian Verse* (1940) decided that there is a specific division of poetry, called 'Christian', a division which excludes, great areas of human behaviour (sexual, political, military), and which leaves little room for doubt or exploration. His definition rests upon a clear and even unquestioning sense of the word Christian, and seems to deny altogether (unlike the equally orthodox Eliot five years earlier) any autonomy to literary standards in the task o exploring religion through literature. Of the twentieth centur Cecil writes:

It is an age of doubt, especially among poets. Not many of them write about religion. During the first twenty years of the century little beyond some verses of Mr Chesterton and Mr Belloc remains in the memory together. But since 1918 Christianity has raised her head again . . .

Founder as he is of the modern school of English poets, [Mr. Eliot] combines a revolutionary technique with an Anglicanism as orthodox as that of Donne. His Christianity is superficially a little rigid and joyless. . . . But if not seductive, Mr Eliot's faith is yet compelling; so certain, so heartful, so courageous to confront the dark elements in experience.

(p.xxxiii)

There is no attempt here to appreciate the confluence in Eliot of orthodox belief with great and original poetry; how the faith prompted the verse, or how the poetry illuminated and enlightened the religious understanding. There is no room here for the poetry of doubt, or literature which appeals to the experience of belief which falls short in its confusion. There is a terrible, prim sterility in Lord David Cecil's notion of Christian verse.

Helen Gardner's *Faber Book of Religious Verse* (1972) is set along-side three anthologies of Christian poetry, partly because, in her Preface, Dame Helen seems to imply that her principal concern is with Christian poems, and partly because this book also is primarily concerned with the Christian religion. The distinction to be made is not between religion and Christianity, but between these terms and *theology*. Like David Cecil, Helen Gardner believes that a distinct category of religious verse can be identified in litera-ture, and that its distinguishing mark is commitment or obligation. As, however, this chapter has already indicated, it is not the *poem* but the *poet* who feels such a sense of commitment, and a poem which is deeply endued with Christian doctrine or tradition may be written by a poet who would deny any Christian belief or affiliation. The poems of such a writer cannot therefore be said to be committed to such belief, but they do raise immensely important questions about the universal nature of the relationship between poetry, poetic truth and the claims of religious belief.

And so, having released religious and Christian verse from the limitations of a specific category within literature, it remains now to ask of theologians how they might see poetry and poetic inspi-ration contributing to their task.

2. The real mystery for the believer lies in the connection between what is held and asserted in the language of faith and what is explained and not infrequently smoothed out in the second-order language of belief, that is, the language of theology. Theology is a necessary exercise in determination and definition. In their doctrinal task, 'the great theologians', writes Austin Farrer

> have strained their minds to grasp the actual relations of like-ness in which things stand to God. By this they have been able to determine which are the closest and most appropriate analogies to use about him; and beside this, which aspects of the things compared with him really apply, and which are irrelevant.[24]

But theology is dangerous. To often it tends to prefer the false security of fixed and definite phrases and formulations, and then it either slips away from the mysterious language of living faith, or else it traps faith into a dependence on platitudes and generalizations which, in their very fixity, become hopelessly vague and abstract. Theology needs to be reminded in its quest for the normative, that in faith there is a mystery and a 'secret' which is inexhaustible and irreducible – a secrecy which is to be perpetually reinterpreted and which keeps theology and its definitions continually trembling on the edge of ambiguity and paradox.[25]

Just as poetry, as we have seen, requires religion and draws inspiration from the definitions of theology, so poetry may serve as a necessary reminder to theology of the mystery, hesitation and hiddenness of religious experience. Poets often understand well the nature of 'mystery'. David Jones wrote in his Preface to *The Anathemata*:

> My intention has not been to 'edify' (in the secondary but accepted and customary sense of that word), nor, I think, to persuade, but there is indeed an intention to 'uncover'; which is what a mystery does, for though at root 'mystery' implies a closing, all 'mysteries' are meant to disclose, to show forth something. So that in one sense it *is* meant to 'edify', i.e. 'to set up'.[26]

Poetry is not theology, but it perceives the danger for theology of assuming a direct stance and a dogmatic assurance which is intolerant of hesitation, doubt or uncertainty. The theologian concerned with the matter of belief must also recognize that Christianity is not only *what* is said, but *how* it is said.[27] Thus, aware of the importance of obliquity and indirectness in dealing with the ambiguity and paradox of faith, Emily Dickinson wrote:

> Tell all the Truth but tell it slant –
> Success in Circuit lies
> Too bright for our infirm Delight
> The Truth's superb surprise
>
> As Lightning to the Children eased
> With explanation kind
> The Truth must dazzle gradually
> Or every man be blind –

> (No. 1129)

There is no shortage of New Testament assertions that 'the Truth must dazzle gradually'. 'Behave wisely towards those outside your own number,' says the Epistle to the Colossians, and 'study how best to talk with each person you meet' (4:5–6). A truthful deception or indirection ('Success in Circuit lies') is at the heart of many gospel sayings: 'be wary as serpents, innocent as doves' (Matthew 10:16); 'use your worldly wealth to win friends for yourselves' (Luke 16:9). These are disturbing sayings, and in the same way, poetry disturbs theological certainty, making its signs dangerous, indirect and provisional, reminding us that God is always greater than what is revealed to us, and that the *truth* of Christian believing is more important than its definition as uniquely *Christian*.

Kierkegaard understood perfectly the necessity of obliquity and 'deceit' in religious discourse.

> What then does it mean, 'to deceive'? It means that one does not begin *directly* with the matter one wants to communicate, but begins by accepting the other man's illusion as good money. So one does not begin thus: I am a Christian; you are not a Christian. Nor does one begin thus: It is Christianity I am proclaiming; and you are living in purely aesthetic categories. No, one begins thus: Let us talk about aesthetics.[28]

Austin Farrer was a theologian who was quite capable of talking about aesthetics and understood a great deal about poetry. In his Bampton lectures for 1948 entitled *The Glass of Vision*, Farrer drew a comparison, but also a distinction, between poetry and prophecy. What the prophet says is 'determinate and particular . . . designed to evoke not an exquisite and contemplative realization of human existence, but particular practical responses to God' (pp.127–8). Nevertheless, Farrer continues, 'the poetical character of the prophetic utterance' is not immaterial, since 'poetry, for the prophet, is a technique of divination, in the poetic process he gets his message' (p.128). Thus, what the prophet and poet share is the technique of inspiration. Both, writes Farrer, 'move an incantation of images under a control' (p.129). Yet this is not to confound the two. What draws them together is *inspiration*.

> Poetry and divine inspiration have this in common, that both are projected in images which cannot be decoded, but must be

allowed to signify what they signify of the reality beyond them. In this respect inspiration joins hands with poetry, certainly on the one side: but with metaphysical thinking on the other. Inspiration stands midway between the free irresponsibility of poetic images, and the sober and criticized analogies of metaphysical discourse.

(p.148)

The poet, the religious seer and even the theologian who works with metaphysical discourse, are all inspired. But, as Farrer makes clear in a later essay, 'Inspiration, Poetical and Divine' (1963),[29] the inspiration of the poet need not be concerned in any way with 'the fundamental mystery of divine inspiration'. The difference is ontological, for the divine inspiration which guides prophecy and doctrine is grounded, not on human resources, but upon the belief that the Creator everywhere underlies the creature.

Nevertheless, despite this difference, theology depends for its ontological validity upon a literary understanding, and that is partly why it is frequently misunderstood.[30] For the ambiguities and paradoxes of theological expression should not be battered into slogan and abstractions, but should be recognized as allied to literary conceits, as devices of expression and sources of inexhaustible meanings. Farrer understood this, and he understood how the responsive or creative imagination of the poet has an ability to grasp fresh and profound resemblances and therefore to keep alive the elusive and tricky language of the theologian.

According to Farrer, the poet's task is not to describe what he feels about things, but to describe things just as he feels them. His task is description, and he is best aided in this by the use of metaphor and figurative language. Why is this so? Language may be used in two principal ways – to analyze and to describe. The scientist uses analytical language to break down what he sees into basic parts and patterns. But analysis does not tell us what a thing is like in its individual character: it does not penetrate what G. M. Hopkins (and Duns Scotus before him) called the *haecceitas* or 'thisness' of a creature or object. The descriptive task of language is best achieved by metaphor. Farrer gives the example of a lover striving to describe the mystery of his beloved, and we may offer a familiar instance from Burns; an example of love striving for exactitude of description:

> My love is like a red red rose
> That's newly sprung in June:
> My love is like the melodie
> That's sweetly played in tune.

(Burns's figure is technically a simile, but metaphor and simile bearing the word 'like', while textually different, are functionally the same.)

Poetry, then, and perhaps especially love poetry, is properly not vague and blinded by sentiment and emotion but strives to describe as exactly as possible the beloved object. In the Song of Songs the bridegroom describes in metaphor his bride's eyes, her hair, her teeth, her lips, her neck, her breasts (4:1–7). Farrer's point is that the poet looks at something and sees it, and is at his most creative in perceiving and appreciating things to the point of love.

> And the chief impediment to religion in this age, I often think, is that no-one ever looks at anything at all: not so as to contemplate it, to apprehend what it is to be that thing, and plumb, if he can, the deep fact of its individual existence, The mind rises from the knowledge of creatures to the knowledge of their creator, but this does not happen through the sort of knowledge which can analyze things into factors or manipulate them with technical skill or classify them into groups. It comes from the appreciation of things which we have when we love them and fill our minds and senses with them, and feel something of the silent force and great mystery of their existence. For it is in this that the creative power is displayed of an existence higher and richer and more intense than all.
>
> ('Poetic Truth', pp.37–8)

The poet speaks in metaphor and analogy; theology itself cannot abandon the language of similitude and speak of the mystery of God in the language of science and analysis, for God is no analysable system. The poet is always there to remind theology of this, and of the reticence, obliquity and indirection of its Truth. Theology meanwhile works upon the language of religious faith, straining in its careful way beyond poetic analogy and poetic inspiration 'to grasp the actual relations of likeness in which things stand to God' (p.37). Poetry itself then finds in doctrine and the language of belief a precise means by which to apprehend the human mystery. For are not the divine and human ultimately, inextricably and mysteriously linked?

In *St Paul and Protestantism* (1870), Matthew Arnold recognized that the problem for so much modern Christian theology was its refusal to perceive the 'literary' character of religious language. Its persistence in attributing to it rather a 'scientific' character resulted in a profound problem for any hermeneutic exercise.[31] Chapter 5 of the present book will be concerned with hermeneutics, and with its religious roots. They are roots which go back to Augustine of Hippo, and can be traced through Erasmus, Coleridge in *The Statesman's Manual* (1816) and Matthew Arnold, until the problems of the contemporary hermeneutic debate are reached, secularized perhaps and aware of dislocation and fragmentation, and yet still in the dialogue between text and reader, challenging the limits we set to the self and opening our awareness to a dimension traditionally called religious.

3

The Poetry of the Resurrection

This chapter briefly examines one central element in Christian belief – the resurrection of Jesus Christ, considering some of the difficulties involved in that belief in the context of a number of literary and poetic engagements with it. It is a practical exercise, considering literature inspired by and illuminating doctrine and belief.

It is not in any way intended to be a systematic examination of the critical problems of the Christian understanding of, and belief in the resurrection. Certainly there are problems, arising out of the relationship between an undeniably odd occurrence in history and the continuing claims of religious experience; philosophical problems about what is going on when we interpret the ancient texts which bear witness to the resurrection; doctrinal problems about the variety of understandings of atonement, a Christian theme inextricably linked with the events of Christ's death and resurrection; historical problems concerning the 'facts' of the matter. I cannot claim to have solutions to any of these problems. I simply want to suggest a way of thinking about them and about the resurrection as central to Christian believing which may provide, for some, a useful aid to reflection.

How far is it a proper question to ask whether the resurrection is fact or fiction? Historically it is such an odd and unlikely event that it might seriously be suggested that 'history cannot establish the facticity of the resurrection'.[1] Furthermore, is the resurrection a 'fact' about Jesus, or his disciples or ourselves and our experience? Is it simply a fact about the past, or about the present and even the future as well?[2] And if factuality is so difficult to pin down, how seriously should we take fiction? Popularly it is usually regarded as the opposite of fact, and therefore untrue or 'made up'. Story-telling, nevertheless, is a very serious business, and imaginative writing makes serious claims upon us. Iris Murdoch has called the creative writer an *essential* truth-teller and defender of words. For D. H. Lawrence, 'the novel is the book of life. In this sense, the Bible is a great confused novel', while Coleridge identifies the logic of poetry as more severe than that of science, 'more difficult, because more subtle, more complex, and dependent on more, and more fugitive causes'.[3] I suggest therefore, that there is value in regarding the resurrection by the criteria of fictional imaginative writing, and that poets have often truly discerned the mystery that theologians somehow miss.

The urge to tell stories or create fictions, it may be said, arises out of a basic need to perceive some consequential order in the confusing chaos of human history and experience. Certainly the Bible, which Blake called 'the Great Code of Art', presents a paradigm of history, a familiar model which begins at the beginning and concludes with a vision of the end. It has a clear plot which starts with the Fall in Eden, and moves towards a restoration in Christ. The Book of Revelation, a late-comer to the biblical canon and still distrusted by some, fulfils the necessary fictional requirement of an ending to the story. For, as Frank Kermode writes in *The Sense of an Ending* (1967):

> Men, like poets, rush 'into the middest', in *medias res*, when they are born; they also die *in medius rebus*, and to make sense of their span they need fictive concords with origins and ends, such as give meaning to lives and to poems. The End they imagine will reflect their irreducibly intermediary preoccupations. They fear it, and as far as we can see have always done so; the End is a figure for their own deaths.
>
> (p.7)

I want to focus this sense of an ending in the biblical model of history, in the first instance not upon the primarily prospective Book of Revelation with its final cry of 'Come, Lord Jesus!', but upon the primarily retrospective event of the resurrection. This is a strange element in a historical story – the life of Jesus of Nazareth, which has a beginning in his birth and an end in his death. It is strange because it is bound to Jesus' death, and therefore to the most fundamental human fear of ending and extinction. But in history this sense of an ending is transformed in the resurrection – the greatest fiction of all and a radically new model of history.

The ending is now also a renewal and a re-creation. In its imaginative audacity, the resurrection is not to be judged by the criteria of the old age of fallenness, but itself stands in judgement upon that age and ushers in the New Creation for those who have eyes to see. The end is no longer an imaginatively predicted future which fails to salve our present fear of death, but is now a strange and disorientating presence 'in the middest', an 'elusive, enigmatic quality, always probing and unsettling, working in our language'.[4]

Poetry and art is well qualified to explore this strangeness, since it is well aware of how language and concepts shift, always inadequate, needing to be modified and re-established, never, as it were, directly transcribing its referent, but transcending it even while remaining bound to its temporal occasion. The elusive power of the resurrection as a 'fact' which lies between past, present and future, between Jesus, the disciples and ourselves, fracturing dogma and definition, is caught with characteristic energy by Lawrence when he defends the importance of the novel:

Religion, with is nailed-down One God, who says *Thou shalt*, *Thou shan't*, and hammers home every time; philosophy, with its fixed ideas; science with its 'laws': they, all of them, all the time, want to nail us to some tree or other.

But the novel, no. The novel is the highest example of subtle interrelatedness that man has discovered. Everything is true in its own time, place circumstance, and untrue outside of its own place, time and circumstance. If you try to nail anything down, in the novel, either it kills the novel, or the novel gets up and walks away with the nail.[5]

Equally, if you nail Jesus to a tree, you either kill him, or he gets up and walks away with the nail. Equally, too, Christian truth, like the truth of the novel, must be appropriate to place, time and circumstance. It cannot be subject to the alien impositions of false historicism, church authority or nostalgia.

Yet, though the elusive truth of the writer's art illuminates something of the strangeness of the risen Lord, the resurrection mystery is subtler still, for Christ nailed to the cross is both killed, and there is a sense in his ending of a new beginning, at once a continuation of and yet entirely unlike that which went before. It is crucial to recognize the strangeness of the biblical encounters with Jesus after his resurrection. Cleopas and his friend on the

Emmaus road fail to recognize the man whose face must have been so familiar to them, until the significant moment of the sharing of bread (Luke 24:31). Mary Magdalene mistakes her beloved Lord for the gardener (John 20:15). Jesus, risen in the body, comes to his disciples through locked doors (John 20:26). The disciples, after fishing, come to recognize the Master in the familiar shared meal of bread and fish (John 21:13). It seems that their relationship with Jesus had to be re-learned in a new life which followed the pattern of the old. But the Last Supper alone was not enough until the same action of a shared meal was repeated in the presence of Christ crucified and risen.

> And the end of all our exploring
> Will be to arrive where we started
> And know the place for the first time.
>
> (T. S. Eliot, 'Little Gidding')

We turn, then, to the logic of the poet, at once subtle and complex, and dependent on more, and more fugitive causes.

George Herbert in his poem 'Easter' recognizes the strange evasiveness of the risen Lord:

> I got me flowers to straw thy way;
> I got me boughs off many a tree:
> But thou wast up by break of day,
> And brought'st thy sweets along with thee.

Here is a very different Jesus from the one who entered Jerusalem riding on a donkey, his way strewn with branches. He has slipped away from his would-be worshipper, not to be approached, but rather comes himself bringing his 'sweets'. The tomb, then, would be found empty at the break of day, so that, as in the Gospels themselves, the central event, the resurrection itself, is missed and not described. Here scripture, poetry and history are all silent, at least until the apocryphal Gospel of Peter, which can hardly be dated earlier than 150 A.D.[6] Ironically, this writing which contains a graphic account of Jesus's exit from the tomb, adds no weight of evidence to the doctrine of the resurrection of the body, since its theology is notoriously of a docetic cast.

At this central moment of the story, language dissolves and

history moves into eternity. What is left is the empty tomb from which the women fled in terror (Mark 16:8). On the one hand, the relationship between the two apparently separate strands of 'evidence' for the resurrection – the empty tomb and the appearances of the risen Lord – is critically extremely difficult.[7] On the other, I do not see how an empty tomb can be adduced as proof of Christ's risenness, or, in the context of the Gospel narratives, as expressive of anything much beyond the inarticulacy and sense of loss of Jesus's followers. Later, in the context of the resurrection appearances, the tomb's lack of a body might perhaps suggest an encounter with a Jesus who is bodily present.

But beyond these deserts of supposition, I prefer to remain with the evasive mystery of Herbert's poem. It is not the event of the resurrection, but the Lord's gift of 'sweets' which is recorded. In Herbert's day a 'sweet' was primarily understood as a sweetened wine or liquor, and here, perhaps, is suggestive of the recurrent eucharistic imagery of the resurrection narratives. Where the elements are shared as a memorial to him, there the risen Lord is present and recognized. In his poem 'Love' (see also above, p. 19), Herbert describes the Eucharist in an encounter between a traveller and his Host, 'quick-ey'd Love', identified in the final stanza as the Lord.

> And know you not, sayes Love, who bore the blame?
>   Me deare, then I will serve.
> You must sit down, sayes Love, and taste my meat:
>   So I did sit and eat.

'Jesus said, "Come and have breakfast." None of the disciples dared to ask "Who are you?" They knew it was the Lord. Jesus now came up, took the bread, and gave it to them, and the fish in the same way' (John 21:12–13).

If George Herbert catches the subtlety and elusiveness of the event of the resurrection in his poems, others have embodied in verse the great drama of redemption which is enacted in the narrative flow of the Passion and Easter. The Scottish poet William Dunbar (1465–1520) powerfully recounts Christ's Harrowing of Hell:

> Done is the battell on the dragon blak,
> Our campioun Chryst confountet hes his force;
> The yettis of hell ar brokin with a crak

> The signe triumphall raisit is of the croce,
> The divillis trymmillis with hiddous voce,
> The saulis ar borrowit and to the blis can go,
> Chryst with his blud our ransonis dois indoce:
> *Surrexit Dominus de sepulchro.*

Dunbar's poem dramatizes that moment of resurrection upon which history is silent. The great fact of Jesus's rising from the dead is imaginatively evoked in the drama of redemption; mere doctrine is remade in a visionary play which finds us, in Coleridge's words, in the depths of our being.[8] Spenser celebrates that same drama more sweetly in his sonnet from *Amoretti* (1595):

> Most glorious Lord of life! that, on this day,
> Didst make thy triumph over death and sin;
> And, having harrowed hell, didst bring away
> Captivity thence captive, us to win.

On Easter Day we celebrate the event of the resurrection, and we are now part of that event; the love which overcomes the restraint of the nails becomes a characteristic of our own restored lives.

> So let us love, dear Love, like as we ought;
> Love is the lesson which the Lord us taught.

In poetry too, is celebrated the new creation achieved by the resurrection – that restoration, by God's grace, of fallen man which St. Paul describes: 'For if the wrongdoing of one man brought death upon so many, its effect is vastly exceeded by the grace of God and the gift that came to so many by the grace of the one man, Jesus Christ' (Romans 5:15). Familiarity has, perhaps, clouded the splendour of Charles Wesley's poem:

> Finish then thy New Creation,
> Pure and spotless let us be;
> Let us see thy great salvation
> Perfectly restored in thee
> Changed from glory into glory
> Till in heaven we take our place,
> Till we cast our crowns before thee,
> Lost in wonder, love, and praise!

The new creation of the risen Lord is at once perfected in him, and awaits completion in us, who have been saved and yet still look for our final salvation and restoration. The tone and pace of the verse alters and quickens with the word 'changed', moving forward and rising with the repeated 'glory', and the expectant, repeated 'till'. Finally we are drawn by its movement to the breathless pause on the word 'lost', at the very edge of language and sense, enveloped wholly by the mystery of God. Wesley's poem captures something of the profound change which is effected in us at Easter, yet which explains nothing systematically. It leaves us, nevertheless, not the lost, confused souls of the old age, but the worshippers of the new age, lost, rather, in the contemplation of the one who has found and saved us.

I have tried as far as possible to let the poetry speak for itself. I should not wish to dispense with the proper processes of enquiry into the evidence for the resurrection in history and in our understanding.[9] But I am equally anxious to avoid what Professor Nicholas Lash describes as the 'empiricism' which draws a simple and clear line between brute 'objective' facts and merely 'subjective' beliefs and impressions.[10] The resurrection sits oddly in history and resists the attentions of many of the criteria of historical enquiry. Equally its 'factuality' in our experience is more than merely insubstantial 'subjective' impressions.

The resurrection is a mystery which slips through human categories of thought, discourse and imagination. Focusing on the cross, that necessary prerequisite of the risen life, Edwin Muir asks:

> Did a God
> Indeed in dying cross my life that day
> By chance, he on his road and I on mine?

> ('The Killing')

At a critical moment of time, the finite and the infinite cross. History is disturbed by a presence which disturbs our history and changes us so that we are never quite the same. History, as history has done since time began, foreshortened that presence by a death and with its ending moved on. But somehow what had ended had also only just begun. The old life indeed was dead, and what is dead cannot be resuscitated. But it could be, and was, restored, renewed; the same yet entirely different. Dostoyevsky wrote of resurrection at the end of his novel *Crime and Punishment* (1866). (This ending is discussed in greater detail below, pp. 104–6). Raskolnikov's punishment for his crime of murder has to be endured, but endured with Sonia and with the New Testament under his pillow, from which she had read the story of the raising of Lazarus to him.

> He did not even realize that the new life was not given him for nothing, that he would have to pay a great price for it, that he would have to pay for it by a great act of heroism in the future.
>
> But that is the beginning of a new story, the story of the gradual rebirth of a man, the story of his gradual regeneration, of his gradual passing from one world to another, of his acquaintance with a new and hitherto unknown reality. That might be the subject of a new story – our present story is ended.

4

Morality and the Text

*'When I say that a great work will inevitably have a profound moral
significance I am thinking of such a significance as will need to be
described as religious too'.*

(F. R. Leavis)

Tom Hughes wrote in the Preface to the Sixth Edition of his novel
Tom Brown's Schooldays (1857):

> Several persons, for whose judgement I have the highest
> respect, while saying very kind things about the book, have
> added, that the great fault of it is 'too much preaching'. . . .
> Why, my whole object in writing at all was to get the chance of
> preaching! . . . if I ever write again, it will be to preach to some
> other age.

(pp.xii–xiv)

Didacticism, the urge to preach, is not uncommon in literature,
even in literature much greater than *Tom Brown's Schooldays*, and
it is not necessarily a bad thing. Ezra Pound confessed, 'I am
perhaps didactic; so in a different sense, or in different senses are
Homer, Dante, Villon and Omar.'[1] But Tom Hughes clearly felt
that *he*, as an author, had a lesson to give and that he was quite
clear what it was all about.

In the face of this claim, what are we to make of D. H. Lawrence's injunction, 'Don't trust the teller, trust the Tale'? The abandonment of a concern for the author and the author's purpose in
writing, has been a major element in much twentieth century
literary critical writing. It underlies T. S. Eliot's 'Tradition and the
Individual Talent' (1919). Much later in 'The Intentional Fallacy'
(1954), W. K. Wimsatt and Monroe C. Beardsley argued that the
design or intention of the author is not an acceptable or even
available standard for the judgement of literature, while most

45

radically, Roland Barthes argued that the author (écrivain), having as his field 'nothing but the writing itself', is ultimately to be proclaimed dead. He is not writing *about* anything, but merely writing (intransitively), not drawing our attention to any thing beyond the writing – as Tom Hughes would claim to do. The writer gives no unitary meaning to the text, for the text is only given meaning as it is read.

What we shall do in this chapter, is examine two very different texts – one an essay and the other a novel, and suggest that the reading of a text may itself be a moral training. Our concern will be with the text as rhetoric and as literary form, quite apart from any didactic intentions of the author or judgements from theological or ethical 'norms'. Let the literature speak for itself. In the absence of the author or even a prevailing orthodoxy, it is not irrelevant to raise moral questions, or to perceive an implied evaluation or attitude towards value within the rhetoric of the narrative.

I

In examining T. S. Eliot's essay 'The *Pensées* of Pascal' (1931),[2] I shall not be primarily concerned with Pascal himself, nor with how accurate or acceptable Eliot is by the standards of Pascal scholarship. Rather I shall examine what the essay reveals of the effect of one writer upon another, the power of the text to exercise a judgement upon its originator and the values embodied in the form, rhythms and rhetoric of the essay. With the text we find ourselves looking at Eliot, and not being led by him by means of the text.

Eliot begins his essay by recounting the few facts of Pascal's life which need to be known when we examine the *Pensées*. Blaise Pascal's character is briefly but carefully drawn and some judgements are made, particularly with regard to his relationship with his sister Jacqueline. His mystical experience on 23 November, 1654 is interpreted in almost literary terms, and also as the result of personal circumstances. 'It is a commonplace,' writes Eliot, 'that some forms of illness are extremely favourable, not only to religious illumination, but to artistic and literary composition' (p.405). Certain kinds of religious experience and the experience of the creative writer have this in common – that the subject or artist becomes a vehicle more inspired than controlling. A writer in this case is not to be judged by his *intentions*, moral or religious, but only by the fruits of his creation.

However, Pascal's writing at this period was far from the mystical. *Lettres écrites à un provincial* (1656–57) are an exercise in religious polemic attacking, as Eliot notes, not so much the Society of Jesus in itself but 'a particular school of casuistry which relaxed the requirements of the Confessional' (p.406). Such use and practice of literary persuasion has a distinguished history, from Demosthenes to Cicero to Swift. Being persuasive, *Letters to a Provincial* have a necessary bias. They are, as Eliot notes, 'unfair', limited and particular. Setting out to achieve a particular aim, they adopt certain literary strategies – the abuse of the art of quotation, for example – to gain their end. As polemical literature they are highly successful, their literary limitations persuading not a theological audience, but the 'world in general' (p.407). The *intention* of the author is here fully realized in the effect of the writing.

The *Pensées* are a very different form of writing. Eliot suggests that Pascal did not find such religious composition easy – an almost tortured expression of what was almost deeper than words. He is careful to define the kind of work in which Pascal was engaged. Pascal was neither a theologian nor a systematic philosopher. He was pre-eminently a scientist, but, more important, a natural psychologist, a moralist and a 'great literary artist'. His style, notes Eliot, 'free from all diminishing idiosyncracies, was yet very personal'. (p.407). His intellectual passion for truth and his spiritual urgency are embodied in a literary style which is finally above the personality and the intentionality of Pascal himself. It is above all, therefore, the fact that he was a 'great literary artist' that makes the *Pensées* so fascinating, morally and spiritually. Our study here is not, therefore, of Pascal, but of his writing and, as important, of Eliot's reading of it.

Eliot's first point is that the *Pensées* are incomplete, merely notes – in Sainte-Beuve's words, 'a tower of which the stories have been laid on each other, but not cemented, and the structure unfinished' (p.407). In other words, it is laid upon the reader to complete the structure, and what is drawn from the text reflects not only upon it, but upon the creative imagination of the attentive reader.

In next describing Pascal's method in the *Pensées*, Eliot predisposes us to a particular form of reading. In order to understand what Pascal is doing we must be prepared to follow 'the process of the mind of the intelligent believer' (p.408). This process Eliot describes in great detail. In proceeding towards faith, the intelligent believer proceeds by rejection and elimination. In the end he finds that Catholic Christianity accounts most satisfactorily for the world, and particularly for the moral world within each person. This ultimate commitment of the believer to the doctrine of the Incarnation, Eliot likens to the 'powerful and concurrent' reasons of Newman's 'illative sense',[3] that is the faculty of judging from given facts by processes outside the limits of strict logic, stressing the creative and imaginative element in faith.

Against this Eliot sets the mind of the unbeliever. And at this point we are caught, unless we are very wary, in the trap of the critic's own prejudices. For Eliot allows his Christian bias to characterize, quite unreasonably it seems to me, the unbeliever as one 'not so greatly troubled to explain the world to himself, nor so greatly distressed by its disorder; nor is he generally concerned (in modern terms) to "preserve values" ' (p.408). The unbeliever is incapable of possessing, apparently, any absolute notion of what is good or bad or, in other words, any absolute moral values. His method is purely inductive, and the great example set up of this method is Voltaire. Pascal's method, on the other hand, which is ultimately rooted in absolute moral values, is 'natural and right for the Christian' and therefore, it would seem, natural and right. Voltaire's refutation of Pascal, if we are to trust Eliot, has become definitive and later opponents have contributed little to the debate. And so, having presented us with the 'method' of believer and unbeliever, Eliot leaves us apparently free to make our choice, for 'in the end we must all choose for ourselves between one point of view and another' (p.409).

But, of course, by this stage in Eliot's argument we are far from free to choose, and our reception of the *Pensées* is already carefully directed. How has our judgement of the literature been affected by the critic? Having at the outset described the incompleteness of the *Pensées* (they cannot speak wholly for themselves), he then creates a framework with his models of the believer and the unbeliever. The moral bias is clearly in favour of the believer, and as Pascal's method is consonant with the mind-processes of the intelligent believer, we are assured that Pascal is basically a safe guide: we become prone to read him in a particular way and complete the fragmentary nature of the *Pensées* according to a particular method, imagining that we are reading objectively and thinking in the spirit of Pascal. The question now to be asked is how far the *Pensées* themselves, as literature, direct Eliot's critical framework, or how much he is imposing upon them. How persuasive is the literature in and on its own terms, quite apart from the doctrinal intentions of the author or the assumptions of the critic? Let us continue to pursue Eliot's discussion.

Eliot has one hesitation in describing Pascal as the 'typical Christian apologist' (p.409). Following an apparently miraculous event at Port-Royal, when a thorn which was supposed to have been part of Our Lord's crown was instrumental in healing an ulcer, Pascal assigned a place to miracles in the formation of faith which, Eliot remarks, 'is not quite that which we should give to them ourselves'. That, of course, begs many questions.

What follows in Eliot's argument is the key to the whole essay. It concerns the relationship of Pascal with the writings of Montaigne (1533–92), through which kinship, 'Pascal is related to the noble and distinguished line of French moralists, from La Rochefoucauld down' (p.411). Eliot suggests that what this tradition has in common is an honesty in the face of the givenness of the 'actual world', its reflections on personal states and moods being 'perfectly objective' (p.412).

Pascal sets up Montaigne as his great adversary. But Montaigne, Eliot notes is almost indestructible.

For Montaigne is a fog, a gas, a fluid, insidious element. He does not reason, he insinuates, charms, and influences; or if he reasons, you must be prepared for his having some other design upon you than to convince you by his argument. It is hardly too much to say that Montaigne is the most essential author to know, if we would understand the course of French thought during the last three hundred years.

(p.410)

Montaigne, or rather the writings of Montaigne, do not persuade like Pascal's *Letters to a Provincial*, by partiality or the limitations of polemic. They influence not so much by what they *say* as by what they *are*, their scepticism more insidious than the arguments and limited incredulity of Voltaire, Renan or Anatole France. They are powerful, as Eliot observes, because the literature is greater than Montaigne himself, its achievement more than Montaigne probably understood, bigger than any individual consciousness (p.411). These writings express a universal scepticism which is the disbelief of every person who thinks, and which may lead to denial or to religious faith.

It is for this reason that Pascal is so powerfully influenced by Montaigne. He opposes Montaigne insofar as his individual doubt threatens to demolish his own faith and endeavours to expose its weakness. But Montaigne and Pascal are at one in their writings insofar as they express an underlying honesty in the face of what is the case. Pascal's own disillusionment is neither distorted nor sick: 'our heart tells us that it corresponds exactly to the facts and cannot be dismissed as mental disease; but it was also a despair which was a necessary prelude to, and element in, the joy of faith' (p.412). Montaigne's writings influence, and find affinity with Pascal, insofar as they are impersonal, universal and, in Eliot's phrase, 'perfectly objective'. The moral power and influence of such great literature – and its quality of greatness arises from its rhetoric and its transcendence of authorial intention – is clear. It does not persuade, it infects the reader.

It is also clear from studying Eliot on the *Pensées* why, as a critic, he was so much favoured by New Criticism. For underlying this deep regard for the text, rather than its author or historical circumstances, is a sense of basic universal agreement and a communal coherence indicating a rich and permanent inherited tradition. This richness denies the possibility of a simple and single vision which would engender a didactic and intentionally polemical literature. It sustains what Terence Hawkes calls an 'ideological commitment to equipoise',[4] avoiding simple and unbalanced involvement. Psychologically its mode is subjective, though the function of literature has been described by Roland Barthes as 'to institutionalize subjectivity'.[5]

The ideological underpinning of such criticism can, of course, be criticized, and Barthes himself has done so most tellingly. The objectivity claimed by Eliot is impossible – or, at least, it is irrecoverable – for neither can the reader confront the words on the page without encountering his own prejudices, nor can we claim that any text exists 'objectively', a signifier clearly tied to its signified. Finally, no critical position is as neutral or universal as Eliot would wish to claim, perceiving a text as expressing the scepticism of *every* human being (p.411). And Eliot betrays his own partiality in the final few pages of his essay on the *Pensées* when he links his comments on Montaigne and Pascal with a specific Christian doctrine, and with Pascal's relationship with the Jansenism of Port-Royal. He writes:

> It is recognized in Christian theology – and indeed on a lower plane it is recognized by all men in affairs of daily life– that free-will of the natural effort and ability of the individual man and also supernatural *grace*, a gift accorded we know not quite how, are both required, in co-operation, for salvation. Though numerous theologians have set their wits at the problem, it ends in a mystery which we can perceive but not finally decipher.
>
> (p.413)

In Jansenism, drawing upon St. Augustine's refutation of the Pelagians, the balance in this co-operation is weighted towards the mysterious workings of grace in the face of the degraded and helpless state of man. The divine mysteries over-arch the petty strivings of the individual, the partiality and the limitations of the aims and purposes of human beings, 'their dishonesty and self-deception, the insincerety of their emotions, their cowardice, the pettiness of their real ambitions' (p.414).

This theological assessment of Pascal and his place in the history of Christian doctrine, has a literary parallel in all that I have been saying; in the limited, partial and inadequate intentionality of the author, and the persuasive and effective power of the text ('essentially bigger than the individual's consciousness' p.411). The mysterious workings of divine grace making for salvation can perhaps be seen in the autonomous activity of the text, in the art of the text by which alone the writer's aim and intention can be judged; in the words of Wimsatt and Beardsley:

> The [text] is not the critic's own and not the author's (it is detached from the author at birth and goes about the world beyond his power to intend about it or control it)[6]

But if the thoughts and attitudes of the text are not to be imputed simply and directly to the text's author, this is not to deny the necessity of the natural effort and ability of the writer in the achievement of the creative act. Both are required in co-operation to achieve the purposes of literature.

Eliot's reading of the *Pensées* concludes therefore, as his slightly later essay 'Religion and Literature' demands, with a reference to 'explicit . . . theological standards'.[7] The literature is judged from the perspective of a 'religious nature with a passionate craving for God' (p.415). Finally, as he has done so often in the essay, Eliot intrudes by offering a definition of a potential readership for Pascal – a particular group of people with particular requirements from the literature:

> . . . I can think of no Christian writer, not Newman even, more to be commended than Pascal to those who doubt, but who have the mind to conceive, and the sensibility to feel, the disorder, the futility, the meaninglessness, the mystery of life and suffering, and who can only find peace through a satisfaction of the whole being.
>
> (p.416)

Once again, the critic predisposes us to a particular way of reading the literature.

In conclusion, how have we been persuaded in reading Eliot on Pascal's *Pensées*, and what finally has been the agent of persuasion? We have seen how Eliot, from time to time, intrudes upon our predisposition, by offering a highly selective group of facts about Pascal as a necessary preparation for reading his work; by describing favourably the 'typical Christian apologist'; by selecting a readership for the *Pensées*. But to a careful reader of Eliot these intrusions should quickly become obvious and a matter for great wariness. For, as Henry James has pointed out, we need to be highly cautious when we perceive the critic trying to be of practical help to the artist or reader, for his chances of saying anything to Pascal which may be genuinely helpful or improving are low.[8]

But equally, Eliot himself warns us against overemphasising the personality, the views or the intentions of the author. Wimsatt and Beardslee aptly recall a remark of one of Thomas Hardy's rustics: 'He's the man we were in search of, that's true, and yet he's not the man we were in search of. For the man we were in search of was not the man we wanted.'

What, then, are we left with? Simply the autonomy of the text and the informality of the critical process? True to his own demands, Eliot certainly does scrutinize his reading with explicit ethical and theological standards. But where those standards are most unobtrusive, and therefore most persuasive, as in the discussion of Pascal and Jansenism, reading the literature has actually prompted theological discussion and confirmed the doctrine in its own literary terms. There has been no imposition of standards on the literature, nor are the *Pensées* to be perceived as the intentionally-directed, limited and 'unfair' literature of polemic and forensic. The literature is not bound by any doctrinal inhibitions, its literary standards independent of and, in this case merely confirming, religious commitment.

In Eliot's essay, the *Pensées* can be seen directing the critic. We have seen how they prompt him to expose his own Christian prejudices and personal limitations. It is a simple matter for the reader of his essay to identify Eliot's presence, and therefore to become aware of the gap between Pascal's work and its particular effect upon this reader. The gap teaches us about Eliot, but it also establishes the independence of the literature – its ability to expose and draw out the individual reader, and to persuade.

But if Eliot's presence is clear without being dominating, Pascal's is shadowy and elusive. He is present, one might say, only in the 'honesty' of the text of the *Pensées*, that is where they slip through the partialities and demands of the critic. Where the text works freely and without reference to critical requirements or stated doctrine, there we might infer Pascal's presence – not so much his intended meaning as his being, in the same way as Eliot infers Montaigne's being in *his* writings. In the *Letters to a Provincial* Pascal is clearly present in the partiality of the writing, in its overt intentions and its historical particularity. But the *Pensées* only reveal Pascal in his universality, in his greatness not as an individual but as Everyman, or, at the limits of impartiality 'as the type of one kind of religious believer, which is highly passionate and ardent, but passionate only through a powerful and regulated intellect' (p.411).

Although I have never refered directly to the *Pensées* but only through the medium of Eliot's essay, nevertheless we have continually bumped up against them, unavoidably through various levels of mediation. We have been persuaded, and our judgement has been educated, by Eliot's criticism, yet the *form* of his own writing has alerted us to his own partiality. What remains is an influence which is at once elusive, undefined and yet finally persuasive; an influence which elicits the response of familiar Christian doctrines of grace and salvation, which is powerful through familiarity and which remains with us as 'a fog, a gas, a fluid insidious element' (p.411), persuading us of an honesty in the face of the '*données* of the actual world' (p.12). In the end Eliot is right, we suspect, in his conclusions about the values of Pascal as a Christian writer, but not right because he tells us so. The *Pensées* themselves continue to persuade, even at this remove – because we see how they work upon Eliot; from even the brief extracts which Eliot quotes (p.415) which distinguish between the *esprit de géométrie* and the *esprit de finesse;* but perhaps above all from their form, to which Eliot alludes. For they are in the nature of fragments, the first notes for a never-completed work, leaving us to complete them from what they themselves intimate and suggest. In the phrase of S. T. Coleridge, they are 'like the fragments of the winding steps of an old ruined tower'[9] which require the reader to complete them in concordance with the structural demands of the edifice.

Ethical questions and questions of judgement are not irrelevant to technique and literary form. We can never, of course, as some literary critics would wish, entirely dismiss personal, biographical, intentional or historical elements in our response to literature. Nevertheless, the text itself remains as a complex structure with a particular relationship to creator, reader and critic. In the end we trust the tale and not the teller, and it is the tale which professes an enduring and profound moral significance, perhaps, as in the case of the *Pensées*, of such a significance as will need to be described in religious terms, and which has the capacity to rediscover and enliven truths of theology and doctrine – the mysteries of grace and salvation.

II

From consideration of an essay, I turn to another literary form, the novel. In his book *After Virtue: a Study in Moral Theory* (1981), Alasdair MacIntyre describes a novelist, Jane Austen, as 'the last great effective imaginative voice of the tradition of thought about, and practice of, the virtues'.[10] She inherits a rich and by no means simple moral tradition, for if C. S. Lewis has rightly emphasized her profoundly Christian moral vision, Gilbert Ryle has also emphasized her descent from Shaftesbury and from Aristotle. Identification cannot, of couse, be through doctrine, dogma or specific religious beliefs, but rather through a preoccupation which is expressed in the form and nature of her literature. MacIntyre describes it in this way:

> When Kierkegaard contrasted the ethical and the aesthetic ways of life in *Enten-Eller*, he argued that the aesthetic life is one to which a human life is dissolved into a series of separate present moments, in which the unity of a human life disappears from view. By contrast in the ethical life the commitments and responsibilities to the future springing from past episodes in which obligations were conceived and debts assumed unite the present to past and to future in such a way as to make of a human life a unity. The unity to which Kierkegaard refers is (a) narrative unity . . .
>
> (p.225)

It is Jane Austen's virtue of constancy, her moral point of view, which is exhibited in heroines like Fanny Price, charmless but genuinely virtuous, or Anne Elliott in *Persuasion:* but equally it is expressed in the narrative form of her novels – a narrative unity making for the coherence of past present and future and continually reaffirming the possibility of constancy in life in the face of seductive charm or the dangers of pride and prejudice, the dangerous attractions of character and wit.

The *form* of the novel is therefore crucial. In his essay, 'Constancy and Forgiveness: the Novel as a School for Virtue', Stanley Hauerwas writes:

> The novel is not important morally just because, as Trollope suggests in the preface to *The Vicar of Bullhampton*, it has the power to elicit our sympathy and thus change our attitudes. That is certainly no small matter, but the novel is still more fundamentally important. Whatever its effect may be, the novel remains epistemologically crucial, for without it we lack the means to understand a morality that makes constancy its primary virtue.[11]

It is not that the novel explicitly teaches religious or moral truths. Rather, the narrative form of the novel enables us to realize the power of our beliefs and the possibility of unity and constancy in life, and to see the human story not in terms of fragmentation or simple cause and effect but within a whole bounded by a fundamental and inescapable assurance of what is right and true. Narrative, it may be, begins and ends in that truth.

My discussion will centre upon one text, Francois Mauriac's *Le Noeud de Vipères* (1932). It was written following a spiritual crisis in Mauriac's life, and has been described as a 'Catholic novel'.[12] But a great deal of Mauriac criticism, it seems to me, attends less to the literary merit of his work than to its potential as religious propaganda. In attempting to describe the novels, it focuses upon Mauriac himself and his Christian beliefs, specifically his Catholic beliefs. Ultimately such criticism would prevent us from reading the novels at all.[13]

The Knot of Vipers is largely in the form of a letter, written by a man to his wife, and to be received only after his death. Avariciously he is planning to rob her and his family of their inheritance. In a brief preface, before the voice of the dying Louis takes over, Mauriac predisposes us towards him, prepares our attitudes and responses. First, in his own, authorial words:

> The man here depicted was the enemy of his own flesh and blood. His heart was eaten up by hatred and by avarice. Yet I would have you, in spite of his baseness, feel pity and be moved by his predicament. All through his dreary life squalid passions stood between him and that radiance which was so close that an occasional ray could still break through to touch and burn him; not only his own passions, but, primarily, those of the lukewarm Christians who spied upon his actions, and whom he himself tormented. Too many of us are similarly at fault, driving the sinner to despair and blinding his eyes to the light of truth.
>
> (Penguin edn. 1985, p.11)

This is subtle writing indeed by Mauriac. It is the only occasion in the novel when he intrudes as author, dictating the nature of his character, judging, and directly guiding the reader in his response. Further, he sums up the life of his character in almost clearly pronounced religious terms, more than suggestive of the effect of grace upon the sinner, in Francis Thompson's metaphor of 'the Hound of Heaven' which pursues the sinful soul. Finally, as in a parable, he draws the reader into the situation so that, from the start, we cannot stand outside the concerns of the narrative, superior and uncommitted. 'Too many of us are similarly at fault.'

This necessary, though brief, authorial intrusion establishes us within a particular yet ambiguous moral attitude even before Louis' narrative begins. But as important is the brief quotation from St. Theresa of Avila, which Mauriac places at the head of the whole book, before his preface.

' . . . Consider, O God, that we are without understanding of ourselves; that we do not know what we would have, and set ourselves at an infinite distance from our desires.'

There is nothing personal here, and no intrusion. Mauriac has not spoken, and we have not yet encountered Louis, to apply these words to him. We feel their truth because we feel it in ourselves. Automatically we have begun to play the role which the miserly Louis will play in the book – our judgement of him will be, to some degree, a judgement of ourselves. And the point of Theresa's remark is that we are divided from ourselves.

The moral pivot of *The Knot of Vipers* is Louis' inability to understand himself – the letter to his wife becomes a confession, his miserly revenge on his family becomes the context for his resistance to religious faith, justified to no small extent by his relations' nominal and institutionalized Christianity. The literary method of first person narrative denies to the reader the direct guidance of the author, but insists on value-judgements because, the preface having drawn us into the dilemmas, Louis' confession and struggle towards self-recognition consists of a series of statements or even just questions which cannot be seen for what they are except in a setting of values.[14]

From whence, within Louis' narrative, do these values begin to be established? Unattractive, avaricious though he may be, the *honesty* of his developing understanding of himself excludes and lays bare the inadequacies of religious conventions. On Good Friday he refuses to fast with the rest of his family.

I like to make a point of eating my cutlet on this day of penitence – not out of bravado, but just to show you that I have kept my will-power intact, that I am not prepared to yield on a single point. . . . With the rest of the family fasting on beans and salt-fish, my Good Friday cutlet will serve as a sign that you don't stand a chance of skinning me so long as there is breath in my body.

(p.43)

He derides the religious platitudes of his wife.

Instead of delivering a frontal attack on your beliefs, I did all I could, no matter how trivial the circumstances, to show how ill your practice squared with your faith. You must admit, my poor Isa, that, good Christian though you were, I had an easy enough task! You had forgotten, if, indeed, you had ever known, that charity is synonymous with love.

(p.80)

First, then, his action on Good Friday was not just deliberate naughtiness. It has a serious purpose, to keep the 'will-power intact', to preserve, in other words, Louis' character; and character is shaped ultimately by beliefs which are ethical and ontological, moral and spiritual.[15] Louis' narrative is the necessary articulation of his character in terms of the preservation of moral stature and self-realization, and both are concerned with avoiding or over-coming evil, whether moral or ontological. It is also the discovery of the nature of that evil, and therefore also of the nature of what is good. It is necessary for Louis to expose the disjunction between his wife's religious practice and the faith which she claims. It is not simply cruelty, since his confession, the honesty of his narrative, requires him to preserve himself in the face of such dishonesty, to move through the terminology and doctrinal requirements of such Christian conventions to a rediscovery of meaning in funda-mental words like love, evil and good. This the narrative, the literary text, unhampered by the limitations of religious practice and belief, absolutely demands.

The increasing pressure of the form of the confession on Louis continually calls him back from partiality and vindictiveness, from his own intentions, to the larger questions.

There, I'm letting my temper run away with me again. I'm back at the point where I left off. I must trace this evil mood of mine to its source, must recall that fatal night . . .

(p.32)

What is the precise nature of the evil that is eating at his soul and the primary source of that jealousy which begins with his wife's confession of an unfulfilled romance which had taken place long before her marriage? But equally mysterious and undefined is the indentification of Louis' goodness by the young Abbé Ardouin, a priest with an ambiguous relationship with the church – his love of music and brief exposure to the secular delights of the theatre had caused his ordination to be delayed – a man whose piety and churchmanship are not quite in accord.

> . . . he took my hand and uttered the following extraordinary words. It was the first time that anything of the sort had been said to me, and I don't mind confessing that I felt knocked sideways.
> 'You are' he said, 'a very good man' . . .
> 'You can't know, Monsieur L'Abbé, how comic that sounds.'
> (pp.84–5)

For a while the two men endeavour to give definition to the word 'good' in terms of Louis' life – in identifiable moral actions, by reference to biblical demands. They fail, though Louis admits in his letter to his wife that she would have been surprised 'if I had told you that the presence of that frocked priest somehow brought me peace of mind'.

Louis' increasing awareness, through the form of his narrative, of the mysterious context of good and evil for his life is occasionally particularized in way familiar within the Catholic background of the novel. In particular the self-sacrifice of his beloved little Marie, shouting in her delirium 'for Papa! – for Papa!' (p.98) exemplifies the idea of 'mystical substitution' (Lodge, p.7). But Louis' self-understanding actually develops in spite of the 'temptations of Christianity' (p.114), in terms of the demands of his narrative and his articulation of his own motives and actions. To his wife, honesty dictates that he confess the 'secret string which Marie could touch merely by snuggling into my arms' (p.114). And in a startling moment he identifies the knot of vipers, his heart poisoned by the evil which encircles him, with Christ struggling and fighting for truth; 'I am come to bring not peace but a sword'.

His poisoned relationships with Isa, his wife and with his family both define the truth of his character, and yet prompt the semi-articulation of a larger truth which only the Abbé Ardouin, in the simplest terms, ever properly recognizes. Looking at the face of a young girl which reminds him of the dead Marie, Louis admits:

> I could feel, almost within reach of my hand, and at the same time infinitely distant, the presence of an unknown world of goodness. Isa had often said to me: 'You never see anything but evil – you find it everywhere . . . 'That was true . . . and yet, it was not true at all.
>
> (p.150)[16]

That 'is/is not', affirmation and denial within the texture of Louis' narrative is his recognition and confession of St. Theresa's observation in her address to God which prefaces the book. He is a man divided from himself, a man whose ostensible life is one thing, but yet impelled mysteriously by a truth and by a standard which is inescapably part of the fabric and form of the text. Indeed, if God does not exist, then the demand is great that the fiction invent him (and inventing, find him to be true). At the height of his anguish and self-contempt Louis cries:

> It has taken me sixty years – I thought – to 'create' this old man now dying of hatred. I am what I am. I should have to become somebody else. . . . Oh God! . . . Oh God . . . if only You existed! . . .
>
> (p.159)

We create the persons whom we are perceived to be. The fiction – the artistic creation – alone is freed from the lying demands and conventions of life and its religions (The equation between literature and life is after all only a modern critical heresy. See below p.87), and keeps true to nature and the ultimate demands of what is true and good. Religion, it may be, is rediscovered in the imperative of the story. For Louis, his confession draws him to a final recognition at the point of convergence between language and silence, life and death.

> 'My child . . . ,' I began, but could find no words for what I wanted to say. . . . Something, as I sit to-night writing these lines, is stifling me, something is making my heart feel as though

it would burst – it is the Love whose name at last I know, whose
ador . . .

(p.199)

But the novel does not quite end with the death of Louis or
with his incomplete manuscript. His son Hubert, the principal heir
to his fortune, writes a letter to his sister Genevieve on his
discovery of their father's 'confession'. He writes of the effect of
the document upon him.

> There is another point of which this narrative lifts a weight from
> my conscience. It is something about which I have long indulged
> in heart-searchings, though I have never succeeded, I must
> admit, in altogether ridding myself of a pricking sense of guilt.
> I refer to the efforts we made – though they came to nothing –
> to get the view of a specialist on the subject of father's mental
> condition. . . . Well, my dear Genevieve, this note-book,
> especially in its final pages, provides ample evidence that the
> poor man was suffering from intermittent delirium.

(p.202)

Hubert's words throw into question the moral effect of the narrative. Within Louis' narrative we have learnt to regard Hubert in
an unpleasant light, grasping, greedy and unscrupulous. Louis
certainly prepares us to be revolted by Hubert's letter. We have
learnt to relate to Louis through his confession, drawn into what
may be called the 'honesty' of his progressive self-awareness. The
sense has grown in us, that Louis' attitudes, even, perhaps, his
goodness (as identified by the Abbé Ardouin), are genuine and
true. Hubert's intimation that this may be so engenders in him a
'pricking sense of guilt', a reflection of his own moral turpitude
in relation to his father. The alternative is to reject the truth of the
narrative, maintaining his own self-righteousness, and simply to
regard Louis' confession and sense of grace, as the ramblings of
a madman.

Has the narrative sat in moral judgement on Hubert? Has its
unity and coherence of form, its structural closure even, so created
an ethical coherence in the life and experience of Louis, that the
reader is persuaded of the substance of its categories of good and
evil, truth and dishonesty – that Louis has indeed been touched
by that 'Love whose name at last I know?' The shaping of the

fictional narrative has perhaps brought about a rediscovery, even a reformulation of the categories and forms of religious belief. Nevertheless, the narrative does not dictate; and its closure is never final; it insinuates and demands a response. Indeed, like a parable, it judges us by our response, as it judges Hubert. By his standards he could not maintain the truth of the narrative. Our final image in the novel is of Louis' grand-daughter, Janine, whom Hubert and his sister keep from believing in her grandfather or from reading his confession. Hubert writes to Genevieve:

> I am delighted to know that you have better news of Janine. I don't think that her excessive religious devotion which makes you uneasy need be considered as a serious danger. . . . Her natural sense of proportion will reassert itself. She belongs to a race which has always known how not to misuse the *really good things*.
>
> (p.205)

The final irony. We are left to judge what the really good things are, a judgement for which we are prepared, of course, by Mauriac in his brief preface to the novel, it may be in his Catholic bias, and by two characters in Louis' narrative, Hubert and Janine, commenting on the narrative. But, as with Eliot's essay, the role of the author in persuasion needs to be carefully qualified, for the narrative is not simply the author's own, but, embodied in language, it belongs also to the reader; and above all its consistency and the fact that it 'works' depends upon its right relationship with those general truths – Kant may have called them 'noumena', ideas of 'God', 'Self', 'Freedom', and so on – which make life intelligible, and which are not known cognitively but are direct reflections in our souls of the Divine originator.

It may be that Mauriac's Catholicism, without doctrinal or moral intrusion, provides that sense of wholeness and unity which Macintyre requires for the virtue of constancy and for a sense of right and wrong. But equally, the narrative itself may be independent confirmation that moral and religious truths are here being sustained. In the words of Professor Hauerwas, 'if we lack a narrative that makes it intelligible to think of each human life as a unity, then in fact we lack the means to make intelligible our confidence that our lives can acquire a story'.[17]

*   *   *

What may we conclude from this examination of two different literary forms, an essay and a novel? Much of the discussion of this chapter has turned upon the issue of intentionality (an issue which continually surfaces throughout this book), and the limited value of assessing the author's intention in the discernment of the moral and religious implications of a text. A literary artifact, a text, whether its form be that of an essay or a fictional narrative, persuades and insinuates itself into our sensibilities in more subtle ways, in and on its own terms, by its form and by the fact that any piece of literature is finally created and complete only when it is received and responded to by the reader.

Good or great literature is most effective in its recognition of the reader's response in the task of making intelligible those values which give meaning to life or by which our lives can acquire a story, a sense of constancy, continuity and unity comprehending more than we immediately desire or deserve. It works on us not only by what it *means*, but also because of what it *is* – its shape, its devices (irony, metaphor, allusion). Its power to affect and persuade is, it seems to me, mysterious and ultimately beyond the grasp of author or reader fully to understand. In discussing Eliot's essay. I likened the autonomous activity of the text to the mysterious workings of divine grace. With it we co-operate, as author or reader, for salvation, its boundaries an ultimate truth and goodness which we recognize but only dimly perceive.

5
Beauty, the True and the Good

We move now from a discussion of the moral and ethical implications of a text to a consideration of aesthetics – the role of beauty
in the matter of the relationship between literature and religion.
This central portion of the book progresses under the three heads
of the Kierkegaardian triad of the aesthetic, the ethical and the
religious.[1] The manner and approach of this chapter will be in
contrast to the previous one, being overtly historical (in its
consideration of Kant), philosophical and theological. It may seem
at times rather abstract. But it will serve to illustrate that there are
many ways to explore the complex borderland of human thought,
imagination and belief which is our subject.

Turning our attention to aesthetics, we come to attend to *form*
in a serious, intellectual way. It is an awesome task since, in the
words of Hans Urs von Balthasar, 'Beauty is the last thing which
the thinking intellect dares to approach, since only it dances as an
uncontained splendour around the double constellation of the true
and the good and their inseparable relationship to one another.'[2]
From this attention to form one can then turn, as we looked at
two literary forms in the previous chapter, to the ethical – the
reuniting, in a refutation of Plato's division of aesthetics and
morality, of the aesthetic judgement with the ethical claims made
by a text in the tradition of Aristotle's *Poetics*, which demands a
recovery of ethics in poetics. Finally, as we shall come to see, the
religious, or more specifically the theological, align the ultimate
concerns and interpretative possibilities of textuality with a
religious framework as an idiom both requiring and embracing the
aesthetic and the ethical.

I

Coherent and systematic consideration of aesthetics has not been common in the twentieth century. In 1923, C. K. Ogden and I. A. Richards explained it in this way.

> Many intelligent people indeed have given up aesthetic specu-
> lation and take no interest in discussions about the nature or
> object of Art, because they feel that there is little likelihood of
> arriving at any definite conclusion. Authorities appear to differ
> so widely in their judgements as to which things are beautiful,
> and when they do agree there is no means of knowing *what*
> they are agreeing about.[3]

Decisions about what is beautiful, or how to distinguish good art from bad, it seems, are necessarily subjective and lack the authority of proper universal criteria. Unsatisfactory and even dangerous are the suggestions of Tolstoy in *What is Art?* (1898), which are overtly Christian. In Tolstoy's argument theology uses works of art to justify itself, and there is a preoccupation with the *content* of a work – the assumption that content can be clearly separated from the form. Such religious imperialism, far from contributing to a real understanding of the value of art and literature, reduces them to a role purely subordinate to theology and belief. Dr Johnson, perhaps, would not have altogether disapproved.

But in a different vein entirely, was a critic like the Hungarian Marxist philospher Georg Lukács in *The Theory of the Novel* (1920) any more successful in overcoming the dilemma expressed by Ogden and Richards? For Lukács, fresh from his discovery of the philosophy of Hegel, was, in his own words, 'looking for a gena-eral dialectic of literary *genres* that was based upon the essential nature of aesthetic categories and literary forms, and aspiring to a more intimate connection between category and history than he found in Hegel himself'.[4] He was well aware of the need to estab-lish universal criteria of aesthetic judgement and of the values inherently residing in forms. The difficulty, as Lukács perceived, lay in establishing a true relationship between these essential aesthetic values and the changing contingencies of the historical and the particular, of comprehending 'permanence within change and of inner change within the enduring validity of the essence' (p.16). But, in the tradition of idealism and the interpreters of

Hegel, Lukács' effort tended towards extreme abstraction and led frequently to arbitrary intellectual constructs. Aesthetic speculation took on an air of refined unreality, and one of the results has been the reaction against aesthetic speculation expressed by Ogden and Richards.

Are we left with these two bleak alternatives: a Christian theological criticism imposing its will regardless of the forms of beauty; or the philosophic intellect spinning its web regardless of the contingencies of time and place?

The positive response of this chapter is based upon a twofold belief. First, that the ground occupied by philosophical aesthetics in the nineteenth century (and everything should be traced back ultimately to Kant's *Critique of Judgement* of 1790) is now being explored by the discipline of literary criticism, and that the new methodological toughness of that discipline combined with a concern for the specific interpretation of texts has gone far to overcome the problem encountered by Lukács and the idealist tradition. Second, the monumental achievement of Hans Urs von Balthasar has unavoidably brought beauty back into the arena of serious theological discussion, and at the same time has recommended to theology the centrality of form as well as content in the business of perceiving and interpreting, and (what literary criticism has rightly recognized at least since the New Critics), the inseparability of form and content in a work of art. The meaning of a text, or for von Balthasar of the figure of Jesus Christ, is in some sense 'in' its structure or 'revelation-form'. Thus von Balthasar entitles the first volume of his Theological Aesthetics, 'Seeing the Form'.

II

It has been suggested that from the *Critique of Judgement* (1790) to Hegel's *Aesthetics: Lectures on Fine Art* (1823–29), we may trace a transition from rational philosphy to something closer to what we would now term literary criticism.[5] On the face of it, Hegel might seem a more reasonable starting-point for our discussion. However, it was Kant who inaugurated the tradition of aesthetics in its modern form, who identifies the fundamental problems in aesthetic judgement, and who, in his third Critique, finally directs his thinking towards theology through his extended consideration of aesthetics. With him, therefore, we begin.

It was only at the very end of his life that Kant came to perceive the serious philosophical implications of aesthetic judgement, and while in many ways the *Critique of Judgement* provides a keystone for the two earlier Critiques, it is the work of an old man, often faltering and inadequately argued. But it is not my intention here to offer a detailed commentary on Kant's work. My remarks, rather, will reflect his thinking insofar as it bears specifically upon our literary and theological concerns.

Kant gives to the basic problem of aesthetics the structure of an 'antinomy', the 'antinomy of taste'. How can the subjective experience of beauty command objective or universal consent?[6] The term 'aesthetic judgement' would seem to be contradictory, since it cannot be at once aesthetic (a subjective expression of experience) and a judgement (claiming to be universal). Upon this very paradox Kant bases his aesthetics, and at the heart of his definition of the beautiful is his emphasis on the *disinterestedness* of the aesthetic judgement (*Critique*. p.50). Although the determining ground of the judgement of taste cannot be other than subjective, its disinterestedness preserves it from those appetites and desires (even good desires) which divide us from other people and even from ourselves. Furthermore, *interest* – when something is deemed, for example, good or bad – implies a prior concept, and to see beauty implies no prior conceptualisation of the object. In Kant's own words, 'delight in the beautiful must depend upon the reflection on an objective precursory to some (not definitely determined) concept'.

This avoidance in judgements of taste of determinate and invariable norms has important consequences for literary interpretation. Such judgements, for Kant, are 'merely exemplary' because necessarily demanding 'the consent of all to one judgement, which can be considered as the example to a general rule that one cannot assert'.[7] (Critique. p.81). Such indeterminacy is first of all a means of relating the general and the particular, for the 'public meaning . . . always only fulfills and determines itself in the particular judgement of taste and in the particular work of art'. Second, the exemplary and undetermined has a dynamic character, that is, in Kant's words, 'further determined through each new concretization'.

Thus it is that our aesthetic judgements are exercised in a context of 'free' beauty – a beauty purified of all interests, tied to no definite purpose, released from prior demands of meaning or function, open and dynamic. It should be said that for Kant, this free beauty is most readily exemplified in nature and not art. The unity perceived in the beauties of nature may not in itself be purposive, but in Roger Scrution's words 'it reflects back to us an order that has its origin in ourselves, as purposive beings'.[8] This experience, leading us to see each object as an end in itself, Kant calls 'purposiveness without purpose'. Aesthetically we come to a perception not of what is, but a perception 'as if'. We are obliged, necessarily, to see the world as if it were thus in order that we may find our proper place in it. Thus, the judgement of beauty free from prior moral conceptualizations, actually frees us to think constructively and engage fully in the moral life.

But before the discussion edges into the ethical (and ultimately the theological), let us pause and consider how it relates to much contemporary discussion in hermeneutics, the study of interpretation, and literary theory. For it should now be clear that Kant's argument for the disinterestedness of the judgement of taste is essentially *formalist*. Even if examples of free beauty abound in nature, they are not absent from art, and the capacity of art to give pleasure apart from a prior commitment to concept or meaning, is through the form or structure of its constituent parts. Kant, it would seem, claims the identification of beauty with disinterestedness and that therefore *form alone* is the essence of the beautiful. True to the fundamental principles of formalist criticism, the work of art, and in particular the literary work of art, should be seen as autonomous (disinterested), and demanding examination in and on its own terms. We should regard the work as form rather than as a series of references demanding extrinsic, systematic judgements.

But, having acknowledged that judgements of taste are, for Kant, 'merely exemplary', it may seem odd that the *Critique of Judgement* is almost entirely lacking in examples or specific images. Indeed, its extreme abstraction contributes considerably to its obscurity and difficulty. Yet precisely this lack of specific images in the writing points us away from specific objects and defined forms to Kant's central concern, which is the activity of the mind. From Kant's third Critique there emerges a central curiosity in Romantic writings with the creative mind, and in particular the creative mind of the artist. In English literature we see it most clearly in Coleridge's 'Dejection: an Ode';

> O Lady! we receive but what we give,
> And in our life alone does Nature live.

The essence of Kant's epistemological system is self-consciousness. Despite his immensely important effort in this Critique to establish the universal validity of judgements of taste, the problem he identified as the antinomy of taste – the dialectic in the act of perception between objective and subjective – and as the unknowability of 'things in themselves', became matters of insecurity for many people in the nineteenth century. In England, for example, it could be argued that Matthew Arnold's failure properly to understand the Kantian tradition resulted in profound insecurity, a despairing retreat from subjectivity and fear of what he saw as Romantic obsessive introspection.[9] What is suggested here is that twentieth-century developments in structuralist literary theory as perceived and qualified theologically in the work of thinkers like Paul Ricoeur (discussed in detail below in Chapter 8), has re-established a firm basis for a proper understanding of Kant's achievement in aesthetic philosophy, and opened up genuine possibilities for a theological aesthetics.

It remains, very briefly, to indicate that in the second part of the *Critique of Judgement*, which is devoted to teleology – an understanding of the end of things – Kant moves through his discussion of aesthetics to a moral sense, and to an intimation of both the immanence and transcendence of God. Drawing upon Edmund Burke on the sublime, Kant's aesthetics become a kind of prelude to theology, for, becoming aware of our own limitations before the grandeur of creation, we realize through the practical reason (whose moral sphere 'legislates for itself alone' and is self-subsisting) that the true end of all creation is in an ideal world, intimated through our moral actions.

This universal judgement of the sublime stretches beyond the limits of language. Kant asserts that language can 'never get on level terms with an aesthetic idea'.[10] This limitation encourages the belief that religion is a matter of interpretation and discovery. In his third Critique, Kant said 'All our knowledge of God is symbolic' and that to take it literally or demonstratively is to 'Fall into anthropomorphism' (p.223). What this suggests is not only the importance of interpretation and interpretation theory, but also the importance of *form* or design as a continuous entity, dynamic in character and open to interpretative development. The form is self-subsisting with an inheritance of fixed, permanent dimensions. The common ground here is occupied by theology which is concerned with thinking about God within particular cultural and linguistic contexts,[11] by the creative artist who deals with formal representations and structures, by formalist criticism broadly defined, and finally by the church which, in Mary Warnock's words, 'exists as a continuing institution (or form) because it is the repository of the word of God, of that symbolism which it must both teach and help us to interpret'.[12]

III

In my discussion of Kant it was suggested that aesthetically we come to a perception not of what is, but a perception 'as if' (see also below, p.106). At this point we are led back to Aristotle's theory of *mimesis* or representation. In his *Poetics*, Aristotle suggests that literature, and particularly tragic literature, does not merely copy or imitate nature. Neither is it simply dealing in illusions or appearances, mere 'fictions' of a world that never was and never will be. It is, rather, an imitation of what is essential to the nature of things and reality itself, a completion and fulfilment of nature. Through its forms and structural organization, indeed, as we shall see, through the structures of *intertexuality*, it imitates an action which is never so complete in nature or experience.[13]

This artistic organization may be described in a variety of ways. Paul Ricoeur calls the 'kingdom of the *as if*', 'the kingdom of fiction'.[14] What is here paradigmatic is emplotment, the 'organization of the events' – as Aristotle describes it – so that imagination and interpretation in effect constitute historical reality, and essentially complete it. Stephen Sykes, on the other hand, prefers the term 'routinization' to describe the artistic representation (in the gospels) or the institutionalization (in the church and its sacraments) of Jesus' activity. This routinization is not simply a decline from a primitive and axiomatic purity. Indeed, as interpretation it is necessary, and it is perfectly possible to distinguish between successful and unsuccessful forms of routine. Professor Sykes puts it in this way:

It is *un*successful when the charismatic potential of the original movement is lost. Under these circumstances one may speak pejoratively of mere ritual or ritualism, and mean that the aspect of *communitas* . . . has been overlaid by the rigidity of the structures in which the rituals are administered. In Christian history there are numerous examples of how the sacred history of Jesus and his disciples, retained in the baptismal and eucharistic rituals, has constantly inspired new charismatic protest against structure and hierarchy, the Franciscan movement and the Protestant reformation being two prominent instances.[15]

Though the instances are not literary, the point should be clear. Continuous interpretation brings about a constant reconstruction of the horizon of expectations – the past is forever being drawn into the present, and in new forms successfully protests against the decayed rigidity of dead structures. The judgement is aesthetic, but also moral and essentially theological.

What needs to be bridged, and most crucially for Christianity with its roots in history, is the gap between the historical and the aesthetic. It begins in the simple recognition that history is inadequately served by attempting what Hans Robert Jauss calls the 'mere annal-like lining-up of the facts'.[16] The historical essence of the work of art lies not in the attempt to imitate or copy but in the prompting of response and interpretation. The strengths and weaknesses of so-called 'reader-response criticism will be briefly remarked upon in the next chapter (See below, pp.89–90). For now we must move the argument on from the dangers of chaotic relativity to potential universality, by suggesting that the literary artifact, primarily by its aesthetic function, is both a product of the new in the process of time and a critical reproduction of the past insofar as it remains of universal significance. The artistic form, therefore, is no simple imitation of what has been the case, but must be viewed dialectically in terms of the formation and alteration of perception. The universal and the temporal together combine properly to influence taste and judgement.

Nor should the matter of response and interpretation be limited to a relationship only between the reader and the work. For there is also a necessary interaction between texts – an intertexuality – forming an historical coherence without any particular claims by any text for originality or primacy. The tradition of the Eden myth moves from Genesis to Milton's *Paradise Lost* to D. J. Enright's

Paradise Illustrated (1978) with, according to strict deconstructive semiotics, no guiding, original intent or stability. While there is logic and value in such destabilizing procedures, their scepticism still must be challenged by the claims of aesthetic judgement and critical theology.

The historical/aesthetic gap as I have described it in terms of Aristotelian mimesis recognizes an interrelation of what we must call, since Saussure, the synchronic and the diachronic (see below p.86). Literature combines a diachronic perspective, reflecting upon the chain of circumstances occurring through time, with a synchronic, giving rise to the sense of an expression of timeless truth. In the literary work time meets eternity, its timelessness guaranteed in the disinterestedness of the aesthetic judgement, free from prior concept or the constraints of linear causality. Yet though the judgement of aesthetic value is made on the universal basis of the timeless truth of great art – Aeschylus, Shakespeare and Wordsworth remain our contemporaries, they never 'date' – such truth is recognized only within a historical context. We necessarily interpret great literature for our own time. And this is precisely why the aesthetic form of literature must have moral consequences. What has been called the 'impurity' of great literature, is a rhetorical aid to interpretation and a recognition that its impassive, objective and timeless purity needs to be rhetorically presented to the reader, and made historically oblique and suggestive, its devices dangerous and making for salvation. In our own literature we have the deliberate fragmentation of Coleridge's 'Kubla Khan', intimating through the device of the person from Porlock a 'dim recollection' of a mysterious whole to which the art merely alludes, the kingdom of the *as if*. In the canon of scripture, it is not often sufficiently recognized that St. Mark's Gospel works so powerfully upon us because it is a carefully structured and artistically refined whole yet seemingly untidy, full of contingencies and random occurences. Disorder and order work together – the form prompting interpretation and decision.

It may be, then, that we are disturbed by the apparent arbitrariness of that Gospel's conclusion at 16:8; by the strange, unconnected incident of the young man in the linen cloth (14:51–2); by the mysterious words of Jesus to his disciples on parables (4:10–12). But our disturbed response to such difficulties is made in the context of the larger careful ordering which resonates through the structure of the book as a whole. For example, the healing of the deaf man with the speech impediment (7:31–7) ought to be balanced with the healing of the blind man at Bethsaida (8:22–6), and both should be seen as commentaries upon the metaphorical deafness and blindness of the disciples, together with the fact that they themselves are 'stammerers' (7:32), that is, incapable of speaking clearly about Jesus. Then immediately after Jesus has healed the deaf, the dumb and the blind, Peter at Caesarea Philippi for the first time perceives clearly and speaks plainly, stating boldly his belief in Jesus' Messiahship (8:29). The seeming chaos of incidents in St. Mark's Gospel belies a careful structuring and balance.[17]

The flawed surface of the literature, as problematic and apparently random as life itself, sets up in us a confusion and a series of responses in the context of a deep, underlying controlled structure. This artistic and aesthetic form has consequences for the reader, morally and theologically. The arbitrary and the mysterious are finally and almost miraculously experienced in a narrative world which does not betray their mystery but which is not, in the end, unfollowable or hopelessly plural.[18]

Art, as I have suggested, is never ethically neutral. The very form of the literary text and the aesthetic judgment which it demands, prompt experimentation with values, even while the author deliberately retreats into ethical neutrality in a poetics intensely concerned with the internal structures of the text. And critics such as W. K. Wimsatt, who have been most insistent that literature should be dealt with as literature and not some other thing, concerned with form and structure, have argued that artistic complexity implies and reflects the moral complexity of actual life. Not that excellence of moral vision in any way guarantees literary or aesthetic excellence, but that such excellence implies and requires moral wisdom. Good literature will therefore have a positive moral tendency and, in the words of E. D. Hirsch in his book *The Aims of Interpretation* (1976), 'by a *structural correspondence*, the moral issue can be accommodated to literary categories' (p.125). Wimsatt, in *The Verbal Icon* (1954), puts it in this way.

The moral value in any given situation, what is right, is abstract; it is known by rule and conscience. By necessity it excludes. Neither a right nor a wrong choice, however, excludes the awareness of many values, some interrelated and supporting, some rival, some sacrificed by a choice, some in situations held in ironic balance or entering into unresolved tensions.

(p.98)

Wimsatt suggests that the poetic and the ethical certainly must not be confused. But that is not to deny, even in the face of the intrinsic strategies of formalist criticism, that a text must imply an acceptable ethical stance if it is to work effectively. Though equally its success is to be judged only in literary and aesthetic terms. Good literature, by its very form and structures, will tend towards a positive morality.

Earlier I referred to the 'Kingdom of the *as if*', 'the kingdom of fiction'. The representation of this ideal in literature is brought about by a re-telling of the story which embraces the flawed texture of experience, its accidents and contingencies, and yet which in its underlying form moves forward to find its fulfilment – a conclusion not necessarily logically derived from what has gone before, but proper to the overall structure of the work. This recognition of what Frank Kermode has called the 'sense of an ending' is the artistic recognition of the paradox of time, in the inter-relationship of the synchronic and diachronic, a recognition of the eternal moment unexpectedly present in the flux of time which moves forward to its final conclusion.

Not simply the story told, but the story re-told – the structural and formal creation of what becomes familiar and well-known – creates an assurance and an expectation to which, mysteriously, the ever-surprising and ever-new quality of the greatest literature contributes. The beautiful is the most familiar, the most mysterious and the most startling. That is why we need to experience repeatedly a *King Lear*, or re-read a *Divine Comedy*, or, above all, the gospels with their message of eternal salvation forever good news for our time. The dialogue in the literary form between the synchronic and the dachronic, the eternal and the temporal, the inchoate and the ordered, derives, it may be, from the pre-narrative and pre-linguistic quality of the experience intimated by the forms of literature, 'an impetus from experience never quite said'.[19] The sayable and the unsayable, the knowable and the unknowable are not exclusive opposites, for there is also, as T. S. Eliot put it in 'The Dry Salvages', 'the hint half guessed, the gift half understood'. The recognition of beauty in the creative mind is a continual process of coming to say and coming to know, which is ultimately a religious quest.

Nor as was recognized in the discussion of Kant's epistemology in the third Critique, is this simply a nihilistic and deconstructive process whereby perpetual interpretation brings about subjective instability and a total loss of the object or primary text. As Frank Kermode in his recent book *Forms of Attention* (1985) puts it:

> The success of interpretative argument as a means of conferring or endorsing value is . . . not to be measured by the survival of the comment but by the survival of its object. Of course, an interpretation or evaluation may live on in the tradition on which later comment is formed, either by acceptance or rejection; but its primary purpose is to provide the medium in which its object survives.
>
> (p.67)

The object survives not with 'objective' meaning, revealed once and for all in the original work, independent of perception in time and history. The task of interpretation, the reading and criticism of great literature, is ultimately the task of a new theodicy, recognizing the necessity of repeatedly deferred meanings, in justifying that which has ultimate meaning in time and in eternity. The final chapter of this book will return to theology and the theme of theodicy in the interpretation of texts and the appreciation of textuality.[20]

IV

Throughout this book I have alternated between theological and literary concerns in a dialectical relationship which refuses to confound the two. In Hans Urs van Balthasar's great *Herrlichkeit*, his six-volume work on theological aesthetics, the crux of the matter is not whether a poet can be defined as 'Christian' or categorized by his belief or worldview, but rather the way in which the poet makes use of the sacred, and how, in series of specified writers (Dante, Hopkins, Eliot, Claudel) a genuine dialogue is established between the divine and the human, the theological and the literary. Dialogue and not identification of the two spheres is the key to the discussion.

This balance will only finally be fully recognized in my last chapter which will suggest the absolute value of literary freedom and the liberation of meaning for a proper theological stance. For the moment, the discussion of von Balthasar must presuppose a clear theological bias, which will be gradually dissolved though not finally rejected, in the critical processes described. In the first volume of his work, *Seeing the Form*, von Balthasar rejects the claims of 'a purely literary analysis', particularly of the New Testament writings, making demands beyond the literary and philological (pp.547–550). He writes that the

> measure of Scripture . . . cannot be accounted for by philological and literary methods, nor in terms of an inner-worldly aesthetics, seeing Scripture's literary and 'well-wrought form', its artistic composition, the balance of its parts, as the criteria for the fact that God is its author, and that it reproduces 'in a worthy manner' the well-wrought form of God's Incarnation. . . . The all-decisive proportion is that obtaining between the form of revelation and the form of Scripture, and precisely this proportion can never be the object of literary scrutiny.
>
> (p.546)

For von Balthasar, the Christian critic must be prepared to accept the charge by structuralist and, indeed, post-modernist criticism of an anachronistic bias if he is to preserve authentic vision, and also he must denounce the tendency to collapse value, to lock all up in the circularity of intrinsic language and the infinite regression of intentionality and meaning. A theological criticism preserves the fundamental principle of a theological aesthetics, that poetic images borne by poetic words establish through beauty the fact of truth and goodness, the distinction between truth and flasehood, and therefore ethically the distinction between good and evil. From aesthetics the discussion will be carried forward to ethics.

But in asserting this bias von Balthasar is careful to affirm that a theological aesthetic begins with no preconception of what is beautiful: it allows the beauty of the divine revelation to establish its own criteria. Indeed, he directly recalls Kant's insistence on the disinterestedness of the aesthetic judgement (p.152). Without preconceptions on our part, beauty is real 'in itself', and not simply real 'for me', its form not to be reduced theoretically into mere fact or ruling principle. It remains free and autonomous, perceived as form undissociated from meaning. Yet beauty is not locked up in the text, and its ultimacy is only completed in the reader. Von Balthasar writes:

> Beauty is the disinterested one, without which the ancient world refused to understand itself, a word which both imperceptibly and yet unmistakably has bid farewell to our new world, a world of interests, leaving it to its own avarice and sadness. No longer loved or fostered by religion, beauty is lifted from its face as a mask, and its absence exposes features on that face which threaten to become incomprehensible to man. We no longer dare to believe in beauty and we make of it a mere appearance in order the more easily to dispose of it.
>
> (p.18)

In response to this, von Balthasar recalls us to an aesthetic perception of form which involves both a beholding and a being enraptured. Theology needs to rediscover the art of looking and of apprehending a text or an object in the fact of its individual existence (see above, p.35) Thus beholding the surface we see into the depths, and becoming conscious of the particular we glimpse the mystery of the universal.

In the first instance such beholding of form must be free of theology – a disinterested reading. The danger of what von Balthasar calls 'aesthetic theology' as distinct from 'theological aesthetics', lies in its dependence upon aesthetic concepts derived from theories of beauty (p.38), or alternatively on dogmatic theological *methods* (p.74) fashioned by 'amateurs' or 'enthusiasts' for their own ends. Against one such method in biblical criticism, the form-critical, von Balthasar launches a sustained attack on the grounds that it anatomizes and dissects the biblical literature, failing to perceive that form is a whole which is greater than the sum of its parts. Truly to perceive the form is to perceive a living organism and behind it something of the creative principle itself.

This raises the question of the relationship, long an issue in neoplatonism, between the notion of the creative activity of God and the creativity of the artist, which I discuss at greater length in Chapter 9. It will be sufficient to make one point here, a point which I will return to later and in more detail in my consideration of deconstruction. Formalist literary theory, as we have seen, has tended to warn us against engaging in interpretation beyond the data of the work itself – the person of the artist or historical circumstance. In terms of strict formalism, therefore, what can we say, from a contemplation of God's 'creation', of the divine creative activity and what it reveals of the 'creating principle' behind it?

Von Balthasar quite specifically recognizes that in any work of art and in the divine creation itself, we can assume no clear intention in the author's mind (p.443). But each in their own way, the artist – God or human – will conceal themselves in their work as much as they reveal themselves. The artist

> . . . becomes unimportant to himself and treats himself as a mere medium which as such does not strive to reach any prominence . . . in God the distances between work and creator are infinite; no natural bridge mediates between them, no ready-made system of expressions of an organic-spiritual kind provides a grammar, as it were, in terms of which an individual work could be spelled out and understood. . . . It is the art of this artist, rather, that in the worldly form which he has invented as his image and likeness, he has on his own initiative also placed and conferred that expressive and revelatory power which allows us to look from this particular surface and understand this particular and unique depth.
>
> (p.443)

We need to see the surface in order to plumb the depths, and thus perceiving the form and grasping its structure, we then begin to recognize what it truly reveals, the mystery, beauty and incomprehensibility of God and all great literature. We can never 'grasp the meaning' of Aeschylus, Shakespeare or Milton, literature which 'constructs' reality as finer than reality could ever be, whose beauty is controlled but also *received* in the endless experience of reading and reception, at which we look and look and yet see nothing. But yet that nothing and the incomprehensibity is not simply a negation. As von Balthasar puts it, 'The more a great work of art is known and grasped, the more concretely are we dazzled by its "ungraspable" genius. We never outgrow something which we acknowledge to stand above us by its very nature' (p.186)

What is granted to the artist and to God in his creative activity is the freedom to create outside rules and aesthetic pre-judgements. But equally what is recognized is the *necessity* in the free creations of art, that they must be just so and not otherwise (p.164). There is an aesthetic necessity which demands the strict givenness of the completed work. To this givenness we must devote a primary attention, in faith, before proceeding with the richness of interpretations which it prompts. 'The Apostles', according to von Balthasar, 'experienced things which they had to accept in their naked factualness, things whose real interpretation was to come only later. It is only subsequently that experience and understanding come together to form one convincing total picture' (p.346).

For the Christian, Jesus Christ is the primary text, the guarantee against the arbitrariness of all aesthetic propositions and value-judgements, and that anything can be said about anything. He is the form expressing God's Being in the world, the object of our contemplation, which to judge is to be judged by. Following Aquinas, a theological aesthetics as we have described it, sees beauty as the *splendor veri* against the aesthetic heresy of art for art's sake, or the moral impoverishment of action without contemplation. The crux of the matter is a genuine dialogue between the divine and the human which incorporates the two principles of reading – that of interpretation and that of valuation. Only thus will we come to recognize our ultimate concern in a fundamental relationship between finite form and the mysterious creating principle itself. The outcome of this relationship is an ethical one, the discernment between truth and falsehood, good and evil. For all our interpretation must recognize itself in the context of the affective and transformative capacity of literature itself, but also of the Christian awareness of human imperfection whereby a theological criticism must determine the moral relationship between the imperfect reader and the text.[21] This will be developed further in Chapter 9.

V

An interesting recent study of the form of religious poetry is Robert Alter's *The Art of Biblical Poetry* (1985). The image of washing away the clogging dirt of theological and historical deposits lies at the heart of Alter's work. For poetry, he contends, is a form of discourse in which the depths are to be perceived in the bright and shining surface. Our response, in the first instance, must be an aesthetic one. In our reading of the Bible, the art of the poetry must be cleansed and released so that, through a careful response to what is there in the text – its formal configurations, its structures, its syntax and overall shape – we recover an engagement with its ancient concerns and power.

The very lack of a recoverable context for so much of the poetry of the Bible allows us to see, without distraction, the power of the language as 'potent performance.'[22] Meaning is not to be extricated from the poetic vehicle, nor is poetry merely a technique for saying powerfully what could equally be said in other ways. Because its form is just so and not otherwise, it has its own imaginative logic making for change in our perception of the world and its creation. Thus typically of Psalm 30, Alter writes that 'the whole argument is tilted along the bias of the poem's medium, language. It is through language that God must be approached, must be reminded that, since His greatness needs language in order to be made known to men'. He cannot dispense with the living user of language for the consummation of that end' (p.135).

And the fact that God's power and beauty is, in part, revealed through linguistic artistry does not mean that God is defined by the artifice of language. Rather, as we have seen (above pp.74–5), the recognition of beauty is a continual process of approach and intimation.

Thus it is that poetry *defamiliarizes*, it moves us by unexpected means to new possibilities and a new vision. In terms of the parallelism of Hebrew poetry, the Russian Formalist critic Viktor Shklovsky has described it thus:

> The perception of disharmony in a harmonious context is important in parallelism. The purpose of parallelism, like the general purpose of imagery, is to transfer the usual perception of an object into the sphere of a new perception – that is, to make a unique semantic modification.[23]

Hebrew verse, based upon a series of parallel statements ('Thy word is a lamp to guide my feet/and a light on my path', Psalm 119: 105), is not just a series of synonyms, the second phrase simply reduplicating the first. The second, rather, develops from the first, strengthening, heightening, 'defamiliarizing',[24] so that the form of the verse carries the reader forward, and attention to the surface logic of the poetry – its imagery, syntax and grammar – leads ever closer to the edge of the mystery. As Yeats put it, we are carried forward by 'Those images that yet/fresh images beget'. The artistic vehicle, far from being simply decorative or attractive packaging for an essential, extractable message, is a particular medium playing a particular and essential role in revelation and religious discourse.

Beauty, and our response to it, is central to the task of theology and religious understanding, central to the attitude of praise which finally characterizes all theological exploration. The power of poetry compels our attention, both exciting our imaginations and also engaging our lives. Its power is a unity, not of logic or ideas, but of aesthetic effect which is finally elusive of paraphrase and rational anlysis, reshaping our experience by claims which recognize the power of form, yet move beyond the purely self-intentive and the non-referential. In my final chapter I shall examine at some length these claims of form and textuality in the context of theodical writings. I shall suggest that a theodicy which seeks to justify the ways of God in a world of evil and misfortune, is in the first instance, to be seen as *text* – not offering rational or propositional solutions, as paraphraseable philosophic arguments, but fundamentally poetic, persuasive by form and the mystery of its aesthetic beauty. And so, the Book of Job remains a profound theodicy in despite of the inadequacy of the solution to the theodical problem in it final chapters. Only when we become aware that fundamental to the text is not only content, but also form and reception, do we realize that the book's adequacy as a literary theodicy depends upon the climactic poetic idiom vouchsafed to God in the closing chapters, richer, more beautiful and more awesome than that given to Job. As Alter puts it, 'through this pushing of poetic expression toward its own upper limits, the concluding speech helps us to see the panorama of creation, as perhaps we could only do through poetry, with the eyes of God' (p.87).

It is only when we are prepared to respond to the artistic power and beauty of perhaps the greatest piece of writing in Christian literature, St. Mark's Gospel, that its perplexing and riddling significance begins to dawn upon us. In the carefully balanced patterning of its parables and miracles there is a system of prefiguration and fulfilment,[25] of concealment and revelation culminating in the account of the resurrection itself which finally hovers on the brink of the greatest of all revelations.

Those much disputed words which conclude the Gospel, 'They said nothing to anybody, for they were afraid' (16:8), are a stroke of poetic genius, leaving us on the brink of the mystery. By parable and miracle we have begun to frame an intuition of the Gospel and the Kingdom, even while parable and miracle remain mysterious by their very subject-matter. But the perception of form, as it is known and grasped in great literature and art, leads us the more concretely to become aware of its ultimately ungraspable genius. And in the final instance, at the resurrection itself, words and courage fail as the great truth dawns. Artistically and aesthetically, the author of the Gospel was absolutely right to conclude as he did.

This point of closure and revelation prompts a decision. Those who remain outside, seeing with the eyes of unbelief, remain simply dazzled by the mystery and its beauty. They look and see nothing, trapped in their own relativities and logical dissolution. But the very mystery of beauty suggests that concealment and illegibility must be recognized in the limitations of our perception; that the mystery prompts a decision, so that with the eyes of faith we learn to read *as if*. By faith, the brink of mystery becomes the textual incarnation of the Divine. George Steiner describes it in sacramental terms.

> Where we read truly, where the experience is to be that of meaning, we do so as if the text . . . *incarnates* (the notion is grounded in the sacramental) *a real presence of significant being*. This real presence, as in an icon, as in the enacted metaphor of the sacramental bread and wine, is, finally, irreduceable to any other formal articulation, to any analytic deconstruction or paraphrase.[26]

As the notion of theological aesthetics has been presented, the literary form and image both bring before us the fact of truth and goodness, and demand that we read, if we are truly to read at all, with the eyes of faith in what is beautiful. From aesthetics and aesthetic judgement we move to ethics and ethical judgement, in the same way as we saw how Kant, in the *Critique of Judgement* moves through his discussion of aesthetics to a moral sense and the ideal which is intimated through our moral actions.

6
Hermeneutics, Literary Theory and the Bible

'The question I have put to myself is: how is this text, the Hebrew Bible, different from all other texts? Is there a basis to the distinction between fiction and scripture? Can we discriminate the two kinds by rhetorical or textual qualities, rather than by external criteria that remain mysterious? To call the Bible a sacred text is to set it apart . . .'[1] That is my initial question in this chapter: my enquiry will focus upon the nature of certain rhetorical or textual qualities in literature, and will be in the nature of a lengthy excursus, returning to the question with, I hope, a degree of enlightenment, only at the very end.

I

John Milton 'wrote up' Genesis, chapters two and three, in twelve books and some 12000 lines of poetry. He read his Bible, and the result was an exercise in intertextuality: not the imposition of a scriptural imperialism on Milton, nor even primarily the creation of a great poem, *Paradise Lost*, but the establishment of a creative interaction between texts, each making the other exist. (A poet, after all, is a ποιήτης – a maker.)

> The world was all before them, where to choose
> Their place of rest, and Providence their guide:
> They hand in hand, with wand'ring steps and slow
> Through Eden took their solitary way.

> (*Paradise Lost*, XII, 646–9)

Milton's fellow poet, Andrew Marvell, thought that he had done a good job in 'unfolding' the vast design of the biblical story.

> And things divine thou treat'st of in such state
> As thou preserves, and them, inviolate.

('On Paradise Lost')

Dr Johnson in the eighteenth century, as we might expect from our earlier discussion of his criticism, was less enthusiastic about Milton's epic. For, the essence of poetry, as he wrote in *The Life of Waller*, is invention: that is, in the modern critical terminology, it defamiliarizes – produces something unexpected, surprises and delights. But sacred subjects cannot be defamiliarized, for they are absolute to faith not patient of human ingenuity, selection, elaboration and alteration. The perfection of the Supreme Being cannot be improved upon or amplified by mere poetry (see above op.10–12).

What presumption, therefore, was Milton's! From *Paradise Lost* the reader 'retires harassed and overburdened,'[2] for the poet, in choosing such a subject has over-reached himself. Such creative comment on Holy Scripture is disallowed, for, Johnson insists, '(religious) truth allows no choice (to the poet), it is, like necessity, superior to rule'. In transgressing the permitted boundaries of expression, Milton has brought about a disjunction between his intention and the effect of his poem, merely frustrating his reader. Blake picked up the hint in *The Marriage of Heaven and Hell* – Milton, far from achieving what he intended, was 'of the Devil's party without knowing it'.

Christian Theology, therefore, according to Dr Johnson, 'too simple for eloquence', stands superior to rule, apparently beyond creative comment. Milton's naughtiness is perceived in the undesired effects of his poem. But let us now move on to an intertext of *Paradise Lost*, and, therefore, also of Genesis. In *Paradise Illustrated* (1978), the poet D. J. Enright[3] 'recreates' the work of Adam in naming the beasts.

> 'Come!' spoke the Almighty to Adam,
> 'There's work to do, even in Eden'.

'I want to see what you'll call them',
The Lord said. 'It's a good day for it'.
'And take your thumb out of your mouth',
He added. (Adam was missing his mother.)

(I.p.9)

Adam takes to his task readily; he has found his vocation. 'He said: "I think of words, therefore I am".' But his task is no simple one, as it turns out.

'I gave him a very nice name,'
    said petulant Adam.
'I called him SNAKE.
I even gave him a second name.
I called him SERPENT.
There's no gratitude in the world,
They bite the hand that feeds them'.

(xxiv. p.32)

Like Milton, apparently, Adam never quite achieves what he intends. You give this beast a very nice name – 'snake', call him 'serpent' even, and the words which began with the best of intentions, turn ugly and abusive – you SNAKE! Language is tricky stuff, a deceiving art; Enright parodies Milton's epic ending: 'The words were all before them which to choose.'[4] But is language, therefore, like Johnson's God, divinely beyond criticism or interpretation?

II

We have come to rest in a problem of language – a linguistic difficulty. It is simply a fact that the main developments in Western literary theory and the theory of text-interpretation (hermeneutics) in the twentieth century, are based on the work of a Swiss linguist, Ferdinand de Saussure (1857–1913) deriving particularly from his lectures delivered in Paris between 1907–11 and published posthumously in 1915 as *Cours de linguistique générale*.[5] It would also be true to say that English-speaking theology has become increasingly aware of the possibility that linguistic analysis and the philosophical analysis of language from the point of view of its logic could lead both to clearer statement and fresh insight. For the moment I will confine myself to a brief introductory look at the work of Saussure, leaving until a little later the question of the relationship between a Biblical hermeneutics and a general hermeneutics conceived as the question of what is understanding in relation to text-explanation.

Saussure insisted on the importance of seeing language from two points of view – the synchronic and the diachronic. Synchronic linguistics sees language as a living whole, existing as a 'state' at a particular point in time (*état de langue*). Synchronically, language is to be seen as a *Gestalteinheit*, a unified 'field', a self-sufficient system. Diachronic linguistics deals historically with the evolution of a language through time, a continually changing medium, or a succession of language states altered by the ebb and flow of circumstance and history. Saussure's insistence on the synchronic study of language was of momentous importance, since it emphasized the structural as apart from the historical qualities of language – language as a total system. Language, therefore, is seen to have a valid existence apart from its history, in the words of Terence Hawkes, 'a system of sounds issuing from the lips of those who speak it now, and whose speech in fact constructs and constitutes the language (usually in ignorance of its history) in its present form'.[6]

Within the phenomenon of language, Saussure makes a further distinction, between the dimensions of *langue* and *parole*. All language is composed of these two aspects: *langue* – the abstract language-system, an intangible convention: *parole* – its application in everyday situations. The nature of the *langue*, produced by what Saussure calls 'the linguistic faculty proper' (*Course in General Linguistics*, pp.10–11), lies beyond, and determines, the nature of each manifestation of *parole*, yet has no concrete existence of its own, except in the piecemeal manifestations that speech affords. *Parole*, our everyday conversation, therefore, is just the tip of the linguistic iceberg. *Langue* is the larger mass that supports it, and *langue* is to be seen structurally as a 'system of signs', a semiotics, where the word is treated as a sign in a lexical code. Each sign is meaningless except in so far as it is defined by its difference from other signs, the sense being found only in the structure. The individual linguistic sign is characterized by the relationship between what Saussure calls *signified (signifié)* and *signifier (signi-fiant)*. Thus the relationship between the concept of a tree (the signified) and the sound-image of the word 'tree' (the signifier) is entirely arbitrary – a structural relationship of value only within the organizing categories of the larger structure system of *langue*. For Saussure, language (indeed, *each* language) has a distinctive and arbitrary way of organizing the world into concepts or categories.[7]

The words were all before them, which to choose. The revolution in the study of language was profound. How was language – so free-floating, uncommitted and arbitrary, to be recaptured? It was true that the concept of linguistic arbitrariness was not a new one. Aristotle had argued that words are not 'natural' but 'conventional', that is socially determined, bearing no relation of similarity to the thing signified. But the doctrine was restated by Saussure in a way that revolutionized the study of language, and so that to a large extent, the old way of criticizing and interpreting literary texts was now apparently invalid. For it had been preoccupied with material extraneous to the work under discussion historical circumstance, the biography and intention of the author (we have already seen in Milton how easily authorial intention and effect can separate), and the place of the text within 'literary history'. But how patient was language of such external constraints, *parole* being merely the tip of the iceberg of *langue?* What were words – signs mischievously free from the things signified – up to with all their linguistic devices of irony, metonymy, and metaphor? Critics accordingly began to work upon the criterion of textual autonomy, and that literature should not be judged by reference to criteria or considerations beyond itself. A poem, or a literary text, consists not so much of a series of referential and verifiable statements about the 'real' world beyond it, than of the presentation, and organization of a set of complex experiences in a verbal form.[8] (Actually, Philip Sidney in his *Defence of Poetry* of 1595 knew very well about the disjunction of literature from 'reality'. The equation between literature and life is in some respects a modern critical heresy.) For the structuralist critic, the interpretative task involves a close analytic reading without drawing on information or material outside the work. Thus, in T. S. Eliot's words, an apparently 'free-floating' uncommitted critical intelligence directly confronts the unmediated 'word on the page'.

Meanwhile biblical critics, all too often, tend to be engaged in projects favoured by literary scholars a century ago, when editors looked for apocryphal passages in Chaucer and Shakespeare, or sought to reconstruct the original *ur-* form of *Sir Gawain and the Green Knight*. Much good it did them!

The formalist critical belief that the form and content of a work are inexticably linked, and the insistence on the text and nothing but the text, were a response, and a proper response, to the implications of Saussurian linguistics, and to the recognition of the power of language. But what are the results of such interpretation theory? The primary result can, I think, be seen in a particular instance of writings of I. A. Richards, a Cambridge critic, whose *Principles of Literary Criticism* (1924) is a landmark in structuralist thinking. Taking up Saussure's relationship between the sign (signifier) and the thing signified, Richards recognizes the purely arbitrary connection between the sign and its material object, *denies that there is any connection at all*, and postulates instead a perfect continuity on the basis that through repeated association, the sign, or word, comes to take the place of the thing signified. (*Principles of Literary Criticism*, pp.127ff) Cutting short, Richards' highly complex argument, we might say that when we read the word 'cat' we are conscious of the sign 'cat' inasmuch as it refers back to the cause of this sign. But for such consciousness to be specific, language must create from within itself, and achieve, a spatial and temporal determination: the word 'cat' forces us to construct an entire universe in order to understand it.[9]

For Richards, therefore, *criticism* does not deal with any given material object, but with a consciousness engendered by language and the *literary artifact* becomes a self-maintaining, even self-consuming vehicle denying any ontological basis – physically or metaphysically – beyond its own structures. We might compare with this David Hume's remark that 'Beauty is no quality in things themselves; it exists merely in the mind which contemplates them.' And so, we can not longer trust to the referential nature of language, and the text has the effect of a Quaker Oats box. The real box is fictionalized when it bears a picture of a Quaker Oats box, which in turn bears a picture, and so on ad infinitum. The copy in the picture therefore, tends at the same time to confirm the reality of what is portrayed and also to disconfirm its substantiality.

What is there left therefore for hermeneutics and for the interpreter to interpret? A mirage mockingly thrown up by language, a prison-house of words, or, at best, a shifting quick-sand of relativities?

I want to outline three responses by theologians to this apparent impasse in the task of interpretation, concluding most affirmatively with the work of Paul Ricoeur in *The Rule of Metaphor* (1975) and Janet Martin Soskice in *Metaphor and Religious Language* (1985), both of whom take very seriously the developments in language theory which I have outlined, and recognize the value of structuralist analyses of texts (Biblical and otherwise), and yet successsfully acknowledge the existential and historical dimensions of interpretation retaining as the object of their understanding, not the structure of a work, but the referent, or world – perhaps even 'God', the text projects through its structure.[10] (Chapter 7 is a more detailed examination of why I believe that the work of Paul Ricoeur is so crucial in the proper development of the relationship between literary and theological studies.)

III

1. I first refer, very briefly, to the hermeneutic strategy proposed by the English theologian, Anthony Thiselton together with two American scholars, Roger Lundin and Clarence Walhout, as a means of escaping the prison-house of language. They have recently combined to write a volume entitled *The Responsibility of Hermeneutics* (1985). They perceive, as I have done, that contemporary discussion of textuality and hermeneutics generally assumes that language is the locus of meaning. Subsuming earlier epistemological debates over subjectivity and objectivity, language theory has absorbed them into a philosophy of language. Questions about texts are really questions about language and its structures, for what else is a text but 'a piece of language'? (pp.31–2). What then of the signified, the reference of language?

In common with the school of literary criticism called 'reader-response', Thiselton, Lundin and Walhout propose replacing the literature-as-language model with a literature-as-action model. The focus of concern now is the consciousness of the reader in the act of reading. Critics like Georges Poulet and Stanley Fish have made the phenomenology of the reading process their study – the point being, what do you bring to the text as you read it, and is it the text or the reader who defines 'meaning'? The benefits of this, not least for the interpreter of scripture, are twofold. First, it acknowledges – unlike the pure structuralist – the existential and historical dimensions of interpretation. Texts are reunited with cultural and historical circumstance. Second, the active and often self-critical role of the reader in the establishment of 'meaning' (ultimately all reading becomes a hermeneutic activity) denies any single or 'ultimate meaning' to a text, for it has the many 'meanings' readers make as they peruse it. That this is so for a text like *Paradise Lost* is not to deny the teleological context of Milton's epic; as theodicy, the meaning of Creation is invisible, deferred until God gives an Ending and reveals himself. Within a plurality of meanings, it may be that *faith* is a recognition of and a commitment to the deferment of ultimate meaning.[11]

Nevertheless, I have to conclude that the hermeneutics of Thiselton, Lundin and Walhout tends towards a chaotic relativism, laying a heavy burden of responsibility on each reader with precious little in the way of clear guidance in the making of judgements or evaluating a response, aesthetically, ethically, or, indeed, theologically.

2. Rudolf Bultmann is a more familiar figure and more difficult to summarize without misrepresentation. Bultmann's hermeneutic programme rests upon two essential principles. First of all, he simply restates a position articulated clearly by Schleiermacher early in the nineteenth century, collapsing the distinction between *hermeneutica sacra* and *hermeneutica profana:* hermeneutic rules in short were to be systematic and universal. Thus, the privileged status granted to the sacred Scriptures, founded upon a belief in their ontological uniqueness – a belief arising out of a supernaturalist metaphysics – must now be denied. Or, at least, it must be denied in terms of their unconditional authority. Henceforth, the authority of Scripture was to be conditional upon critical procedures. Second, Bultmann was acutely aware of the alienation of the biblical texts, historically and culturally, from the contemporary interpreter, both as a cultural fact and as a methodological principle. This very brief statement of these two principles is not intended as an introduction to a full or balanced survey of Bultmann's hermeneutic strategy. I simply wish to try and fit his demand that a text be demythologized into the context of my present argument.

A universal and soundly critical hermeneutic overcomes the problem of the historical distance of a text from the interpreter for

Bultmann (as for Schleiermacher before him), because the meaning of the text is finally located in the interpreter's consciousness. Schleiermacher put it this way: 'By leading the interpreter to transform himself, so to speak, into the author, the divinatory method seeks to gain an immediate comprehension of the author as an individual.'[12]

Bultmann modifies Schleiermacher by shifting the locus of meaning in a text from the author to the 'subject matter'. Here we reach that difficult word 'myth'. Bultmann does not understand myth as presenting an objective picture of the world as it is. Its intention, rather, is, in his own words, 'to express man's understanding of himself in the world in which he lives', or 'a certain understanding of existence' as it is grounded and limited by the transcendent.[13]

Now the task of demythologizing is not actually so much concerned with myth itself, but rather the relation between words and meaning. For, as Bultmann learned from Cassirer, Heidegger and his own pupil Hans Jonas, language not only expresses, it also distorts. There is a hermeneutical gap between letter and spirit; language – mischievous as ever – impedes and obscures the purpose of myth. To demythologize (or interpret), is to strip away the camouflage of language so that the possibility of existence intended by the myth relates directly with the consciousness of the contemporary interpreter.

In many ways Bultmann foreshadows the more recent developments in reader-response criticism and the whole post-modernist-movement in literary theory, which place a minimal value on the text itself. For, and here is the crux of my complaint against Bultmann, his hermeneutic theory implies a belief in a serious concern which exists over and against, indeed in spite of, the text before us. Texts are at best inadequate guides, and the good interpreter will always be seeking a more adequate expression of the truth which will render the vagueries of Scripture redundant. And so he shifts the question of revelation away from Scripture to an 'event' in the believer's existential self-understanding.

For the structuralist, and indeed post-structuralist, we live bound in the non-referential prison house of language. Bultmann, on the other hand would try to lead us away as far as possible from the camouflage of language. One encounter is entirely intrinsic to the text, the other wholly extrinsic – and each is finally deadly. Is it not possible, after all, to engage in a universal critical exercise, aware of the dangers of avoiding the ontological problems of religious discourse, and to return the locus of revelation and divine meaning to the scriptural texts themselves?

3. The final hermeneutical strategy which I offer, and, potentially at least, the most satisfactory within the critical terms I have set, is that proposed by Paul Ricoeur, and brilliantly echoed by Janet Martin Soskice in her recent book *Metaphor and Religious Language*. Far more that Bultmann, Ricoeur as theological hermeneut is difficult to summarize, since his vast literary output covers a wide range of disciplines, among them history, theology, philosophy and literature, and his writings on the specificity of religious texts are occasional and fragmentary. His most complete statement appears in the periodical *Semeia*, 4 (1975), entitled simply 'Biblical Hermeneutics'. But my primary text in this discussion will be his lengthy study *La métaphore vive*, oddly translated into English as *The Rule of Metaphor*, with the sub-title 'Multi-disciplinary studies of the creation of meaning in language'.

In his investigation of the revelatory power and ontological foundation of religious discourse, Ricoeur insists that it be perceived also as poetic discourse. He distinguishes clearly between poetic language and non-poetic language, indentifying three principal themes in poetic language (*The Rule of Metaphor*, p.209).

(a) Poetic language presents a certain 'fusion' between meaning or sense and the senses. It thus denies the arbitrary and conventional nature of the signs of non-poetic language, which separate meaning from the sensible as much as possible (as in Saussure and also Wittgenstein's *Philosophical Investigations*).

(b) In poetic language, the pairing of sense and the senses tends to produce an object closed in on itself. The sign is looked at, not through. (Ricoeur recognizes the value of formalist literary criticism, as I have described it, with its immanentism and abandonment of the referential function of language.)

(c) This closure of poetic language allows it to articulate a fictional experience, presenting 'an expression of virtual life'.[14]

There is the theory. In a structuralist mode, one sees an awareness of sense – sensitivity: a recognition of the reader's response which, for Ricoeur, may be evidence of poetic meaning at a given point in the text (textual objectivity) but is nevertheless not constitutive of it.

And so, moving to practical, hermeneutic application. The non-referential nature of poetic language denies us the possibility of responding directly to a text with a definitive statement of what it refers to – e.g. 'it is talking about the Temple'. Rather the act of reading prompts the hypothetical, 'I *see it as* the Temple' – half thought and half experience, an *interpretation* forming a hypothesis which one can verify. (Ricoeur here is almost certainly drawing upon Wittgenstein, *Philosophical Investigations*, IIxi, p.194e). Poetic language, then, demands of the reader a particular hermeneutic activity, dependent on language (what Ricoeur would call 'semantic') structure, and necessary for the reclamation of an object of reference.

Let me now narrow the discussion to the process of reclaiming one particular referent which is the special concern of the biblical texts and religious language, that which we designate by the word 'God'. Ricoeur's procedure for interpreting religious (or religious-as-poetic) discourse is as follows. First we should take the text seriously as text in an attitude of 'sympathetic imagination'. Second, we should then engage in a rigorous structural analysis of the *sense* of the text, determining what marks in that sense 'open' the sense to a referent, albeit indirectly and hypothetically. Third, we should lay out the referent of the text as an experience of some nonlinguistic reality indicated by the text.[15]

As we interpret such religious discourse we need to bear in mind that it is not literal (which implies a simple and straightforward relationship with its referent), but metaphorical. Metaphor might broadly be described as a set of processes in language whereby certain characteristics of one object are 'carried over' (μετα–φερειν) and transferred to another object. The second object then is spoken of in the manner of the first. In terms, therefore, of something to which we cannot directly refer, we might ask, how may the kingdom of God be described? Metaphorically is the answer.

But when the poet says, metaphorically, 'nature is a temple where living columns . . .', there is a tension in the verb 'to be' – it both *is* and *is not*, and the power of the metaphorical image depends upon the tension between metaphorical affirmation and denial. Also, this tension, or the inherent inadequacy of all metaphorical language as redescription, demands an extension into further metaphorical ventures which relate to the original metaphor, qualifying, interpreting, correcting.

> 'I am an asphodel in Sharon,
> a lily growing in the valley'.
> 'No, a lily among thorns
> is my dearest among girls'.

> (Song of Songs 2, 1–2)

Metaphor calls to metaphor, so that, in Ricoeur's words, 'metaphor proceeds from the tension between all the terms in a metaphorical statement'. ('Biblical Hermeneutics', p.77). The complex poetic structures in biblical literature function as metaphors and models of redescription, each modified by the presence of metaphorical qualifiers that Ricoeur calls 'limit-expressions'. Limit-expressions, themselves metaphorical, function to 'transgress' or overturn the normal course of metaphoric process, and to 'intensify' its effect so that the forms of language 'converge upon an extreme point which becomes their point of encounter with the infinite' (Ibid., p.109).

Hermeneutic activity, therefore, must attend seriously to metaphorical interaction within a text, and modalities of discourse between texts (intertextuality), and, recognizing that this relational and structural activity is the key to the notion of metaphorical *truth*, propose an interpretation of the ontology thereby implied (*The Rule of Metaphor*, p.295). To put it more particularly and simply, Ricoeur describes the significance of the word 'God' as the point of convergence that gathers together all the referents which issue from the many partial discourses in the biblical canon: it is at once 'the co-ordinator of the varied discourses and the index of their incompleteness, the point at which something escapes them'. ('Biblical Hermeneutics', pp.129–30.) Hermeneutics is an exercise in pluralism, recognizing textuality as almost inexhaustively inventive, impatient of any fixed predetermination (the single, definitive meaning), and in Scripture reflecting the infinite richness of the divine revelation in its multivocality.

And so, before the conclusion of this chapter, I come to a very brief word on the work of Janet Soskice, which illustrates well Ricoeur's thinking on metaphor and religious discourse. Soskice would reject the naive, *uncritical* claim that 'Christian worship is undeniably addressed to one other than the worshippers, a King of the universe who makes all things, knows all things and rules all things . . . a cosmos-transcending absolute being',[16] with all the energy of a theological Don Cupitt (whose words I have, in fact just quoted) or, a philosophical A. J. Ayer. Cupitt and Ayer, as good traditional empiricists, would say that if a claim is to be genuinely cognitive, there must be strictly applicable definition, clarity and certainty. A clear, straightforward account must be given of what it means to say 'God exists'.[17] Such traditional empiricism criticizes all so-called non-literal language, and in the end denies the possibility of any metaphysic. Nor, therefore, can Soskice comfortably accept Cupitt or Ayer.

Slightly more satisfactory than such extremes in Soskice's view, is Ian Ramsey's account of religious language – the account of a philosopher anxious to defend the cognitive in theology, and the metaphysical. The problem is that Ramsey is not enough of a philosopher, nor a good enough critic to make workable his claims for models for divine activity. His claim for the clear objective reference for Christian assertions and 'models' is grounded in 'cosmic disclosure' – 'the sense I have of being confronted, of being acted upon.'[18] The difficulty, as Soskice points out (p.146) is that such disclosure is simply a point of reference with no content – a dangerous naïvity unable to sustain the critical arguments which Ramsey would wish to lay upon it.

Do we then replace cognition with mere emotion – a feeling for God?

Taking the ground I have described in Ricoeur's work, Soskice could argue that theological realism, and the theist's right to make metaphysical claims, is only critically sustainable through a recognition of the power of textuality and the sometimes wayward, sometimes profoundly constructive power of language: through, furthermore, an interpretative hermeneutic strategy which is prepared to live and proceed constructively with metaphorical complexity. Soskice writes:

> . . . we have stressed that it is not our object to prove the existence of God, still less to prove that the models and metaphors which Christians use in speaking of God have a special validity. Our concern is with conceptual possibility rather than proof, and with a demonstration that we may justly claim to speak of God without claiming to define him, and to do so

by means of metaphor. . . . Despite claims to the contrary, a reflective theological realism . . . need not do violence to genuine religious conviction by vulgar anthropomorphism – indeed, it is particularly well suited to a theology which wishes to preserve the sense of God's transcendence.

(p.148)

Only when this fundamentally literary and critical claim has been established (literary because grounded in metaphor which gains life from the texts of scripture), may we very properly turn for sustenance and guidance to experience, community and an interpretative tradition in Christian belief.

*   *   *

'To call the Bible a sacred text is to set it apart . . .' I began this chapter with those words. But if, as Erich Auerbach in *Mimesis* (1946) – that seminal work for modern literary criticism – has suggested, there is something in the sacred text which prompts us towards such a conclusion, or, as S. T. Coleridge claimed in *Confessions of an Inquiring Spirit* (1840) 'in the Bible there is more that *finds* me than I have experienced in all other books put together', then this privilege granted to Scripture must be only on the basis of a radical and critically respectable hermeneutic. This must not take the form of an extrinsic encounter between religious language and concepts appropriate to our present cultural situation, as Bultmann wished, or worse, between religious language and concepts conjured up by inadmissable theological naivity. But the privilege granted to the Biblical text must be hard won, not least through a critical awareness of it as literary art and language. For the Bible, whether we like it or not, is art composed of that tricky stuff language, and, as Iris Murdoch expressed it, seriously, ironically, yet with feeling, in her novel *The Black Prince* (1973), 'Art is not cosy and it is not mocked. Art tells the only truth that ultimately matters. It is the light by which human things can be mended'. (Penguin edn, p.416.)

7

The Limits of Formalism and the Theology of Hope

In my Introduction I suggested that the formal study of Religion and Literature in the United States in the 1950s arose out of, and also as a reaction against that type of Formalism which became known as the New Criticism. For much of the later chapters of this book the tenets of that kind of literary criticism have been near the surface of my discussions. Finally, in Chapter 6, Paul Ricoeur was referred to as a critic, theologian and philosopher who recognizes clearly the value of the whole structuralist movement in literary theory, yet also perceives its limitations and shortcomings in the exploration of the language of theology and belief. It is time now to pursue in more detail the nature of these limitations and my sense of a need for a 'criticism of criticism' which is, I believe, essentially a theological activity. Once again, Paul Ricoeur, and also a theologian to whom he is indebted, Jürgen Moltmann, will be very much at the centre of my argument. My final two chapters will move on into the more radical and questionable, some may want to say nihilistic, area of deconstructive theory as another possible way of ultimately revisiting the mysterious truths of faith and theology.

I

Literary criticism, claimed George Steiner, somewhat romantically, in the first sentences of his book *Tolstoy or Dostoyevsky* (1959), should arise out of a debt of love. Sustaining a high view of the genius of the artist, Steiner suggests that great works of art, the poem or the drama or the novel, pass through us like storm-winds, seizing upon our imaginings and transforming our perceptions: and the truest insights of criticism originate in the attempt

97

to persuade others to lay themselves open to the force of our experience of such art. To the great tradition, the lines of spiritual descent from Homer to Yeats and Aeschylus to Chekov, criticism must return 'with passionate awe and a sense of life ever renewed', and such criticism, engendered by admiration, Steiner calls 'the old criticism' – historically and politically aware, 'philosophic in range and temper', and always referring us back 'a la métaphysique du romancier' (Sartre), looking upon moral purpose. Against this he sets much contemporary criticism which is quizzical and captious; it often comes to bury rather than to praise, to lose all in relativity and self-absorption.[1]

The old criticism, it is true, had its bias, tending to believe, according to Steiner, 'that the "supreme poets of the world" have been people impelled either to acquiescence or rebellion by the mystery of God, that there are magnitudes of intent and poetic force to which secular art cannot attain, or, at least, has not yet attained' (p.14). Steiner notes with approval D. H. Lawrence's words. 'I always feel as if I stood naked for the fire of Almighy God to go through me – and it's rather an awful feeling. One has to be so terribly religious to be an artist' (Letter to Ernest Collings, 24 February 1913). But if an examination of the creative process is forced to look beyond the text to what is transcendent and extrinsic to it, then it may be suggested that the bias lies not so much in the criticism as in the art itself, and criticism's business is to establish the truth or not, as the case may be, but certainly not to deny or avoid it by setting a priori limits to its own procedures.

How far is what is broadly known as Formalism, within which general definition we may include what Steiner calls his 'new criticism', guilty of setting such limits? Formalist literary criticism is extremely wide in its scope, the name Formalism being originally applied to a school of Russian linguists and literary historians of the 1920s of whom Roman Jakobson is the best known. Built on the groundwork of Symbolism, early Formalism was concerned with form as a communicative instrument-autonomous, self-expressive, by rhythm, associative and connotative means able to 'stretch' language beyond its everyday use. Preoccupied with form, the two definitive tenets of modern Formalist literary criticism are the assertion that the form and content of a work are inextricably related, and that therefore the meaning of the text is in some sense 'in' the structure of the work itself. In the early days of American New Criticism such writers as Cleanth Brooks,

John Crowe Ransom, René Wellek, Wayne Booth and Austin Warren wrote in opposition to certain undeniable limitations of 'older' criticism, and in their various ways, argued for the autonomy of art and that it be examined in and on its own terms. They argued for the inseparability of form and content in a literary work.

New Criticism raises serious problems regarding a question which lay at the centre of my lengthy examinations of Eliot's essay on Pascal's *Pensées* and Mauriac's *The Knot of Vipers*. It is the question of authorial intention in a text. By its standards, of course, the author's intention (a factor extrinsic to the text) cannot be normative for interpretation, and formalist critics in general, since Wimsatt and Beardslee (see above p.145), are hostile to the suggestion that knowledge of an author's 'mind' or 'human qualities' is relevant to the interpretation of a given text. But the question of intentionality is a difficult issue in hermeneutics, and even those formalists who deny a normative role to authorial intention still tend to argue that the *text* is intentionally open to other interpretations. Furthermore, it seems to me that pluralism of interpretation cannot be endless, even if it may be virtually so, and the grounds for preferring one interpretation as against another argue for an awareness of some point of reference outside the text by virtue of which the text becomes meaningful. Now, with regard to a text of scripture, for example, this need not presuppose overt dogmatic intentionality on the part of the author, though it may indicate some notion of authorial will (for instance, the sense of the need for a Saviour) as a prerequisite for the analysis of verbal meaning, even though one cannot be certain that the author is fully conscious of the intended meaning.[2] Indeed, precisely insofar as the interpreter makes explicit these intended but unconscious meanings, he may claim to understand the author better than the author himself.

New Criticism's claim, therefore, to be an entirely 'intrinsic' method, and Formalism's aim to achieve the 'total critical act' (such as Georges Poulet claimed had been done by Barthes in *S/Z*), must be seriously qualified and not only in the question of intentionality. It repeatedly calls upon familiar philosophical or religious terms and categories to state its case, and insofar as it attempts to establish a theory to support intrinsic analysis it precisely demonstrates its lack of self-sufficiency. Despite all its claims about the 'sealed and sovereign' context of poetry, the practice of New Criticism may be placed critically in the tradition of Aristotle's *Poetics* which demands the recovery of ethics in poetics and which emphasises not the internal and intrinsic structure of the text, but in Paul Ricoeur's term, 'structuration' as an oriented activity that is only completed in the reader.[3] The aesthetic value of literary autonomy is not necessarily in conflict with the theological value of relevance.[4]

Here we should dispense with one limitation concerning the origin of a moral tendency, that it is purely immanentist, finding its origins in human experience and the simple produce of the common day, what Geoffrey Hartman in his book *Beyond Formalism* (1970) calls in the context of European Romanticism 'second naïveté' (presumably drawing upon Ricoeur's terminology in *The Symbolism of Evil*)[5] – that is an acute perception of and participation in the world. Ricoeur's account of ethical orientation is more profound and more theological than that.

II

Our intention, with Ricoeur, is to establish the usefulness of Formalism within its limitations, while at the same time pointing out the dangers of its claims to completeness. Ricoeur's approach to hermeneutics, it seems to me, incorporates the insights of formalist literary analysis, while at the same time recognising the 'extrinsic' existential and historical, indeed ethical, dimensions of interpretation. It is best discerned in his broad criticism of Gadamer's monumental work *Truth and Method* (2nd Ed. 1965) in his essay 'The hermeneutical function of distanciation'.[6] According to this criticism, Gadamer might better have entitled his work Truth or Method, for it suggest an intolerable opposition between an existentialist notion of truth – ontologically revealed and appropriated, in Gadamer's term, by 'participation'; and a methodology pursued through that clinical 'alienating distanciation' which grounds the objectivity of the human sciences. This distanciation, a standing back in a position neutral to both author and reader, is the 'method' of the New Critic, the structuralist, the formalist. For Gadamer we must choose between truth or method. Ricoeur, on the other hand, suggests not an opposition, but a dialectical relationship (having, admittedly, its own problems in the establishment of what is true) between explanation (method) and understanding (truth) which enables us more adequately to describe the tension between self and other, and to remain responsible to the explanatory methods of the formalist while at the same time preventing epistemology from swallowing up ontology. Language and criticism must not become self-consuming artifacts, but must live, intelligently, in hope. Ricoeur insists upon the ontological foundation of language, and that a text is fundamentally referential; it intends to say something about the world, a world which knows its limitation, in truth.

This project, for Ricoeur, will take place within the limits of reason alone, within the internal exigencies of the terms set by language, To put it another way, George Lindbeck, with whom, in most respects, I disagree profoundly, has suggested that a religion can perhaps be viewed as a kind of linguistic framework that shapes the entirety of life and thought, functioning rather like a Kantian *a priori*, or an idiom.[7] Taking, then the Gospel as text, it is found to speak in the first instance not of that which lies beyond it, of transcendence and of freedom in hope. In the first instance it speaks of truth, and, says John, 'the truth shall make you free'. Ricoeur has admitted to being deeply influenced by Jurgen Moltmann's book *The Theology of Hope* (5th edn, 1965), with its eschatological interpretations of Christian Kerygma. He applauds Moltmann's resituation of the Resurrection as hope for the future within the framework of the Jewish theology of the promise, removing it from the Hellenistic schemas of 'epiphanies of eternity'. Ricoeur writes:

The Resurrection interpreted within a theology of promise, is not an event which closes, by fulfilling the promise, but an event which opens, because it adds to the promise by confirming it. [*That confirmation is important*. D.J.] The Resurrection is the sign that the promise is henceforth for all; the meaning of the Resurrection is in its future, the death of death, the resurrection of all from the dead. The God who is witnessed to is not, therefore, the God who is but the God who is coming. The 'already' of his Resurrection orients the 'not yet' of the final recapitulation. But this meaning reaches us disguised by the Greek Christologies, which have made the Incarnation the temporal manifestation of eternal being and the eternal present, thus hiding the principle meaning, namely, that the God of the promise, the God of Abraham, Isaac and Jacob, has approached, has been revealed as He who is coming for all'[8]

Seeing as it were, the 'text' of the Resurrection as a structured totality and perceiving what it achieves by its form in confirming the promise, this critical 'distanciation' is not simply alienating–an epiphany of the eternal glimpsed in the temporal, the eternal swallowing up the temporal. It is rather productive of potential horizons of meaning, an interpretation of the Resurrection in terms of hope, of promise and of the future. As we shall see in a moment when we apply this discernment of the Resurrection to the final pages of Dostoyevsky's *Crime and Punishment*, at a certain point criticism is recognized as not only ethical, but also philosophical and most genuinely theological. The explanatory methods of the New Criticism serve to explicate the various ways of construction to freedom in hope.

Here allow me a momentary digression. In his book *The Great Code* (1982), Northrop Frye applies to literature Giambattista Vico's concept of the three ages of mankind; the age of gods, the age of heroes, and the age of the people (pp.5–14). Vico describes these as poetic, heroic and vulgar respectively. In the poetic age, pre-Platonic and taking in much of the Old Testament, subject and object are linked with a common energy and there is no distinction between the work and what it refers to or signifies. In the heroic age, poetic harmony is replaced by the 'dialectical logos', language becomes élitist, analogy prevails, and language, having lost its harmonious relationship with its referents, becomes instead the verbal imitation of reality. In the vulgar, or 'descriptive-scientific' age, subject and object are clearly separated and the neutral, observing subject is motivated to examine the objective world. The aim is the discernment of 'scientific truth', the method inductive. Language seeks to be clear and distinct, yielding to close analytic reading and ultimately self-sustaining. Enter New Criticism and the promise held out by I. A. Richards of a convergence between logical positivism and literary criticism. A purely epistemological methodology will, it seems, lead us into all truth.

But it quickly becomes clear, as Paul de Man pointed out in his book *Blindness and Insight*, that this fine aspiration reaches a dead end; that the soulless distinction between subject and object, observer and observed, rapidly disintegrates into interpretative pluralism and disorder signifying ontological complexities.[9]

In I. A. Richard's pupil, William Empson, the scientific claims of formalist criticism effectively evaporate. No friend of Christianity or its theology, Empson nevertheless concludes in his book *Seven Types of Ambiguity* (1930), that true poetic ambiguity proceeds from the deep divisions of Being (with a capital 'B') itself, and that poetry does no more than state and repeat this division. Criticism can analyze this ambiguity, but the conflict having been *named* in the text, the text can do nothing to resolve it. And the nature of the conflict is suggested in an extraordinary statement, coming from Empson, that 'it is at once an indecision and a structure, like the symbol of the Cross'.[10] *Seven Types of Ambiguity* concludes with a discussion of Herbert's poem 'The Sacrifice', which is a monologue uttered by Christ on the Cross, drawing upon the Lamentations of Jeremiah. The conflict, identified by criticism, can be resolved only by the supreme sacrifice which breaks (and confirms) the incarnate (intrinsic) word. Ambiguity and the sorrow of separation are now perceived to have their origin outside the intrinsic form of the text or human artifact, the meaning of the text cannot be said, therefore, to be 'in' the structure of the work, and formalist techniques, in critics like Philip Wheelwright in *The Burning Fountain* (1954), have become overlaid with intentions of a mythical and religious order. Concern for structure is expanded by what Wheelwright would term 'ontological implications', by a concern for origins and the promise of meaning in reconciliation.

Beginning with the positivism of the formalist critic, we move to Empsonian ambiguity and paradox. Does this remain the very essence of the poetic insofar as it remains unresolved? Or do we proceed further towards a reconciliation with a belief in the poetic as a salvational act, from narcissim to hope through the experience of limitation?

In the hermeneutic exercise of Paul Ricoeur, it seems to me, the insights of New Criticism are more positively recognized. Ricoeur defines meaning as inclusive of both sense and reference, and the referential trait in the structure of a text does not sacrifice the semantic autonomy of the text which New criticism demands. A Text is both 'closed' and 'open' – closed as a complex, structured totality which is, on the insistence of New Criticism, objective and self-sufficient. But it is also open insofar as the reader or interpreter, moving 'intrinsically' within the structure of the text, moves through its dynamics from sense to referent – towards the promise which it confirms.

For Ricoeur, and perhaps the New Critics, as I have described them, a literary work does not refer directly to a given reality, but to a 'possible world' created by the syntactic and semantic structures of the text. Giles Gunn makes a similar point in his book *The Interpretation of Otherness* (1979) describing Aristotelian mimesis, when he writes that 'Aristotle was at pains to show how literature, and particularly tragedy, could be said to complete and fulfill nature, rather than merely imitate or copy it, by presenting *through its formal organization* the completed imitation of an action which in nature or experience is never so unified or fully realized' (p.59; my italics).

III

Let me in conclusion, very briefly illustrate what I have been trying to say in this chapter by looking at one significant passage in Dostoyevsky's novel *Crime and Punishment* (see also above p.44). I come to it here because it was suggested by Ricoeur's appreciation of Moltmann's interpretation of the Resurrection (the final great image of Dostoyevsky's book) in terms of hope, promise and future, and because one of Moltmann's finest short meditations on the Resurrection is his essay 'Dostoyevsky and the Hope of Prisoners', which examines particularly *The House of the Dead* and *Crime and Punishment*.[11] The image of the prisoner is a good one for the New Critic, bound within the world of the text, tied to its structures and denied access to extrinsic 'methods' or 'systems'. But, for Moltmann, hope comes to life as the prisoner accepts his imprisonment, affirms the encircling stone walls and bars, and within his situation discovers the real human being in himself and others. Not at the time of physical release, but actually within prison the 'resurrection for the dead' takes place. And so, perhaps, within the formalities of New Criticism, hope is born.

At the end of *Crime and Punishment*, Sonia, the child of misery, follows the murderer Raskolnikov into exile and prison, and, in Dostoyevsky's words 'an inexhaustible sympathy, if one may express it so, lay in her face'. Sonia lacks fear or self-concern; she does not judge, condemn or justify; 'extrinsic' categories of evaluation are absent from her; she simply experiences Raskolnikov's foreboding destiny as her own. And by this Raskolnikov is enabled to abandon his theories about life, his methods and his systems, for life itself. In formalist terms, he begins to live life within 'intrinsic categories'.

And so in the relationship of Sonia and Raskolnikov, the 'already' now achieved orientates the 'not yet' of the final recapitulation.

> Suddenly Sonia was beside him. She had come up noiselessly and sat down close to him. It was still very early. . . . She smiled at him joyfully and tenderly, but, as usual, held out her hand to him timidly . . . now their hands did not part. He stole a rapid glance at her, but said nothing and lowered his eyes to the ground. They were alone and on-one saw them. The guard had turned away at the time.
>
> How it happened he did not know, but suddenly something seemed to seize him and throw him at her feet. He embraced her knees and wept. At first she was terribly frightened. . . . But at once, and at the same moment she understood everything. Her eyes shone with intense happiness; she understood, and she had no doubts at all about it, that he loved her, loved her infinitely, and that the moment she had waited for so long had come at last.
>
> They wanted to speak, but could not; tears stood in their eyes. They were both pale and thin; but in those sick and pale faces the dawn of a new future, of a full resurrection to a new life, was already shining.
>
> (Penguin edn, p.557)

Everything is suddenly taken away from Sonia and Raskolnikov and their relationship is isolated. The incident comes unbidden and out of context – 'Suddenly Sonia was beside him'. The structure of the fiction is immediately self-sustaining, supported only by the play of its elements. It is as if in a play the scenery and all that relates the dramatic action to what is outside the interaction of the characters, is stripped away. The environment, the historical and geographical setting, vanish. A bare spotlight illuminates only two characters, the universe confined in the structures of their relationship and interplay. Nothing is said, no one sees them and the guard has turned away. They do not know how the experience comes to them. But then the indecision and the structure, like the symbol of the Cross, recognizes a projection that is founded not merely in the relation of elements to which all has been reduced.

Its foundation, we recognize, exists not merely in those related elements in the game, which J. Hillis Miller, for example, has claimed as the ontological basis of form in Victorian fiction.[12] As Dostoyevsky concludes his novel, the present story is ended, its structures completed. But their completion confirms the subject of a new story, and 'an acquaintance with a new and hitherto unknown reality'. (p.559).

In conclusion, I return to where I began, with George Steiner, this time in his Leslie Stephen Memorial lecture entitled *Real Presences* (1986),[13] recognizing, even as I write (and as shall be seen in the chapters which follow), a value in the deconstructive enterprise in contrast to Steiner's romanticism. His questions, nevertheless, remain pertinent. Whence may we escape relativity, Steiner asks, the ontological indeterminancy of all value-judgements, for to interpret is indeed to judge? Alas, we may lament the 'autistic echo-chambers of deconstruction'. Are ethical postulates sufficient? No. We must read *as if*. We must read as if axiomatically the text before us had meaning (compare above, p.70).

Can it be that God cannot be summoned back to our agnostic and positivist condition? Or how far behind the abrasive, arrogant contemporary models of criticism and aesthetic judgement lie, in Steiner's word, 'The abandoned, the unpaid-for idiom, imaginings and guarantees of a theology or, at least, of a transcendent metaphysics'? Are we called now to pay up, to recognize the necessity for commitment?

Perhaps living and working with the sad critical logic we have been taught, is, as so often the case, the most unexpected road back to that which we thought we had lost, recognizing here the never-fully-to-be-realized ideal of all interpretation and valuation.

This discussion has illustrated, I hope, how in one particular manner, a serious commitment to literary critical method may, sometimes paradoxically, lead us back to truths which theology has forgotten or has failed to articulate; that the forms of literature and art can often quite spontaneously illuminate in startling ways the divine work of creation and redemption; and that theology, critically and rigorously pursued, in its turn, continues to offer a systematic and necessary reminder of the things of ultimate concern to literature and literary criticism.

8

Beyond Formalism

What I shall say in this chapter may well seem unfinished and somewhat lacking in coherence – indeed it is and deliberately so. Its argument for openness and refusal of closure in texts may seem to contradict, to some extent what I argued for in Chapter 4. I do not wish to deny my claims there. Nevertheless, 'the words were all before them, which to choose', writes the modern poet, aware of his great seventeenth-century predecessor who wrote of a whole world. 'Which to choose' – how do we choose our words; naturally, perhaps, or merely conventionally? Does it matter if, Adam-like, we look at that four-legged creature and decide to call it 'dog'? An arbitrary choice, but at least we have established that it is different from that other four-legged beast we call 'cat'. The difference is established, but the words are no less arbitrary – and God is only Dog backwards, after all.

And here I am writing, putting these arbitrary signs together, like Roland Barthes, unwilling 'to move from the contingency of writings to the transcendence of a unitary, sacred product'.

I delight continuously, endlessly, in writing as in a perpetual production, in an unconditional dispersion, in an energy of seduction which no legal defense of the subject I fling upon the page can any longer halt. But in our mercantile society, one must end up with a work, an *'oeuvre'*; one must construct, i.e., *complete*, a piece of merchandise. While I write, the writing is thereby at every moment flattened out, banalized, made guilty by the work to which it must eventually contribute.[1]

That Final Word – what dangerous status do we claim for it? Transcendent, sacred: – I'll stick with my playful contingency: I'll defer commitment (thank God or something, for Jacques Derrida – differ, defer, *différance*), play with everybody else's beliefs without the inconvenience of adopting any myself, abandon meta-physics. I follow Barthes finding that

> the closer I come to the work, the deeper I descend into writing; I approach its unendurable depth; a desert is revealed . . . It is at this point of contact between the writing and the work that the hard truth appears to me: *I am no longer a child*.

(p.419)

I can no longer live with the uncritical conclusions of what I have simply been told is the truth.

I

What a critical world of tensions and contradictions, of arbitrary relationships and *deconstruction* in fact, we live in! Critical 'deconstruction', or 'post-structuralism', inspired principally by the French psychoanalyst Jacques Lacan and the philospher Jacques Derrida, seeks to demonstrate that any text necessarily undercuts its own claims to a clear, determined meaning. Beginning with Kant, we have come to live with a sceptical divorce between mind and the 'reality' it seeks to understand,[2] and from Kant we move to Saussure – who perceived the arbitrary nature of the linguistic sign – to Derrida, who robs Saussure of the last vestiges of the Western metaphysical tradition. Gone, it seems, is the Romantic insistence on harmony and organic unity, the 'organic' aesthetics which for example, the poets Coleridge and Wordsworth offered in response to the moribund theology of the eighteenth century and Paleyite apologetic. For Coleridge in *The Statesman's Manual* (1816) the symbol 'partakes of the Reality which it renders intelligible' and 'abides as a living part in the Unity of which it is the representative'.[3] Symbols according to Coleridge are 'harmonious in themselves, and consubstantial with the truths, of which they are the *conductors*' (p.29). Nothing arbitrary here – for art, expression, language itself, is properly an organic element in creation, a means of insight into the universal from the particular, and the eternal from the temporal. Words are 'natural' not 'conventional' or arbitrary, and the Bible, in particular, reveals

> the stream of time continuous as Life and a symbol of Eternity,

inasmuch as the Past and the Future are virtually contained in the Present. According therefore to our relative position on its banks the Sacred History becomes prophetic, the Sacred Prophecies historical, while the power and substance of both inhere in its Laws, its Promises and its Comminations. In the Scriptures therefore both Facts and Persons must of necessity have a twofold significance, a past and a future, a temporary and a perpetual, a particular and a universal application. They must be at once Portraits and Ideals.

(pp.29–30)

The Scriptures are portraits of facts and persons, and also ideals because they are portraits. Behind this lurks the venerable theory of mimesis, whose task as we have seen (see above p.104), is to imitate less what is simply an appearance or illusion of reality than an imitation of what is essential or basic about reality itself. Crossing the centuries to Sir Philip Sidney's *Defense of Poetry* (1595) the assumption is maintained that literature should imitate the possible more than the actual. But imitate it must.

Oh, blessed rage for order! That Coleridgean order which conceives of the literary symbol as a 'concrete universal'. Which, deeply romantic, magnifies the mystery of the artist, who, in George Steiner's words 'both imitates and rivals the shaping powers of the Deity'. We think of D. H. Lawrence being so terribly, religious as an artist. Then, it all coheres – utterance and perception, language – the actual – the possible.

Indeed, even Kantian scepticism was offered as an escape route from the radical, sceptical reasoning of David Hume which denied the possibility of any self-validating knowledge of the external world. At least for Kant, knowledge could be *mediated* by the mind as the world's interpreter; not reality unmediated but subjected to regularities – the *a priori* truths of human understanding. And contemporary structuralist criticism does, in a sense, exemplify the Kantian hermeneutic in the emergence of structured habits of reading and literary possibilities. Thus, Jonathan Culler in *Structuralist Poetics* (1975) writes how,

By offering sequences and combinations which escape our accustomed grasp, by subjecting language to a dislocation which fragments the ordinary signs or our world, literature challenges the limits we set to the self as a device of order and allows us, painfully or joyfully to accede to an expansion of self.

(pp.129–30)[4]

But is not the dislocation and fragmentation now beyond recall, leading not to expansion but rather to disintegration and collapse? I believe that the Saussurian development of the theory of the arbitrary nature of signs, has more extensive epistemological and ontological implications than Culler is prepared to admit in this passage.

Saussure's fundamental anti-historicism, as I suggested in chapter 6 (p.86), insists on the *synchronic* as distinct from the *diachronic* study of language – that is, in the words of Frederic Jameson, 'language as total system is complete at every moment, no matter what happens to have been altered in it a moment before. This is to say that the temporal model proposed by Saussure is that of a series of complete systems succeeding each other in time'.[5] Essentially a-historical, language also has a distinctive and 'arbitrary' way of organizing the world into concepts or categories. In Saussure's theory language is a structured *system*, so that our concerns shift from a 'substantive' view of the subject ('what' we are talking about), to a 'relational' one.[6] Are we, we must begin to ask, talking about anything at all, descending into a bottomless ocean of relativities?

I am simplifying, for the sake of brevity, extremely complex issues. The point is that, for many critics, language is now felt to be in a state of crisis. And the crisis, promoted by Saussure, is taken to its extreme conclusions by Jacques Derrida, who has properly identified it as a crisis for that entire metaphysical tradition upon which, like it or not, Christian belief and theology is based. In Derrida's words:

It indicates, as if in spite of itself, that a historico-metaphysical epoch *must* finally determine as language the totality of its problematic horizon. It must do so not only because all that desire had wished to wrest from the play of language finds itself recaptured within that play but also because, for the same reason, language itself is menaced in its very life, helpless, adrift in the threat of limitlessness, brought back to its own finitude at the very moment when its limits seem to disappear, when it ceases

to be self-assured, contained, and *guaranteed* by the infinite signified which seemed to exceed it.[7]

Language is longer *contained and guaranteed by the infinite signified
which seemed to exceed it*. Those are the telling words. For Derrida
there is a failure in Saussure's work to think through the implications of his own mode of discourse. Saussure's insistence on the
privileged status of speech and the spoken word (*parole*) is odd in
a theory so committed to the primacy of language-as-system
(*langue*). The spoken word, as a metaphor of truth and self-auth-
entification rests upon a philosophical tradition centering on the
'living voice', a tradition which is committed to a belief in some
ultimate reality, – a logos, presence, God or Truth – which guarantees and underwrites every thought, and all language and experience. We rest upon an ultimate, ontological surety, a metaphysical
guarantee of sense and coherence.

Against this, Derrida proposes a pure, impersonal theory,
entirely freed from metaphysical clutter. Prior to speech is *writing*
which is personally uncommitted; not writing as graphic, but as
pure *difference* or différance (for a more detailed discussion, see
below pp.119–21). Christopher Norris describes it in this way.

> Writing, for Derrida, is the 'free play' or element of undecid-
> ability within every system of communication. Its operations are
> precisely those which escape the self-consciousness of speech
> and its deluded sense of the mastery of concept over language.
> Writing is the endless displacement of meaning which both
> governs language and places it forever beyond the reach of a
> stable self-authenticating knowledge.
>
> (*Deconstruction* pp.28–9)

Derrida, it should be said, has been out-Derrida-ed by many of
his disciples. He is not the thorough-going nihilist which some
have claimed him to be. But it has to be said that his cold, arresting
and absurd logic challenges the presumption, critical or theological, of a centre or fixed principle; the notion of solid foun-
dations or a formal structure built upon them. Relativities, deferment, différance – the death of certainty, the death, even of God.

II

What then, can we say of literature or theology? Has the course of so-called literary theory, from Saussure and his study of language (the stuff of literature), to Jakobson and the Russian Formalists, to Levi-Strauss and anthropology, to structuralism, to the isolation of the autonomous text in American New Criticism, to Lacan and psychoanalysis, to post-modernism and the radical a-historicism of the deconstructionists (Derrida, Michel Foucault), simply ground literature itself out of sight and out of all existence? Where, in all this, lies our appreciation of great art and our sense of the numinous?

First, I would make the point that the development of literary theory in the twentieth century has been made, not oddly and idiosyncratically, but, upon the basis of the most profound, even traumatic intellectual and socio-cultural movements in Western society in the last hundred years or so. Without Kierkegaard or Nietzsche there would be no Derrida. Indeed, deconstruction must be understood in the context of a European literary and philosophical tradition which begins at least with Kant and Hegel.[8] The transformational theory of Saussure's linguistics – from *langue* to *parole*, from deep structure to surface structure or actual articulation of language – goes back certainly to Marx and Freud, (in Marx's laws of transformation, of slave into wager-earner, and so on: in Freud's transformation from the unconscious of dreams to the language of consciousness).[9] One could go on. Literary theorists have drunk deeply of our political, and intellectual heritage, and its recent upheavals.

Why then this theoretical enquiry into – some would say imposition upon – literature? Let us be quite clear. Theory does not simply get in-between the reader and the work, blurring our response to and appreciation of literature. Rather, theory of some kind is required in the very identification of a literary work, and in learning to read it, and it seems to me that the defining of literature as an intensification of and deviation from ordinary language is inextricably tied up with our system of beliefs, our sense of social, political and cultural context. We cannot read untheoretically, for without theory (however derived, whether from within or without) literature would cease to be 'literature'.

Listen to these words from a Professor of English Literature at Oxford early in this century:

England is sick, and . . . English literature must save it. The Churches (as I understand) having failed, and social remedies being slow, English literature has now a triple function: still, I suppose, to delight and instruct us, but also, and above all, to save our souls and heal the State.[10]

Literature at the turn of the century, it seems, had a religious role in the wake of the Victorian crisis of faith. Literature was read, then as now, against an intellectual and cultural background. Some no doubt would say that the Christian tradition and its theology had lost its authority, its power to save souls, and had run its course. Critics like George Gordon, or Matthew Arnold before him, remained committed, however, to an understanding of literature which was squarely in the tradition of Western metaphysical philosophy – a 'Logos' tradition ('In the beginning was the Word') which was 'guaranteed by the infinite signified which seemed to exceed it'. This fundamental, ontologically rooted anchor we may call by many names – Idea, Self, or, best of all, God. Tied to this base, words all cohere in referential order, language means something and leads us beyond, substantively and bravely into transcendence. Here was no self-referring prison-house of language.

But the system, even then, was collapsing. Could 'literature', thus understood, support the apparent failure of religion after Kant, after Marx, Freud and Nietzsche? The background was changing and the theoretical base was cracking. In our own time J. Hillis Miller, in a classic study, has read the works of De Quincey, Browning, Emily Brontë, Arnold and Hopkins as literature, consciously or unconsciously, confronting a sense of the disappearance of God.[11] The question of theology's 'given' is raised, and something is immediately said about the theological enterprise.

Theology, it might be said, is founded in the face of something more primordial than itself. It is a derivative, responsive and second-order enterprise.[12] If, etymologically, working from and towards God as the sole given is the way of theo-logy, then the effective disappearance of that given naturally results, for many, in the abandonment of theology, dispensable because derivative. But what may seem here to be intellectually honest fails to reckon with the heart, its reasons and its emotional attachments. Literature is perceived as taking over from theology, but does so continuing to play the role it has always played in a Platonic and traditional Western Christian framework. Quite simply, in the words of Northrop Frye in his book *The Secular Scripture* (1976):

> . . . it has been generally assumed that the function of serious literature is to produce illustrations of the higher truths conveyed by expository prose. The real social function of litera- ture, in this view, is to persuade the emotions to align them- selves with the reason, and so act on the 'heart', which perhaps means not so much the pump in the chest as the primary or primitive brain.
>
> (p.24)

This, it seems to me, is essentially the view of critics like Professor Gordon. The religious framework remains, fragile and without foundation, and the social function of literature continues in an even expanded form: but the criticism and critical theory which demands this of 'literature' is empty, facile and without philo- sophical underpinning.

What is needed, of course, is a new understanding of the nature and practice of theology as well as a developed literary theory which can properly embrace the contemporary socio-cultural situ- ation – or at least recognize it.

III

We have seen how literary theory has developed in the recognition of the change of ideas since Kant. Theology too, has sometimes made its adjustments in complex ways, beyond the scope of this brief chapter. Just one, deliberately extreme example of a radical theological movement which recognized in a reading of one particular poet the possible groundwork for a new form of Chris- tian theology will have to suffice as an illustration. Many people, I am aware, would dismiss this example as an unworthy aber- ration, a sordid, forgotten episode. But it does rightly claim its place in the Western tradition, and its shadow is a long one, stretching now into the much-debated world of post-modernist literary theory.

In the 1960s, the so-called 'Death of God' theology looked back to Kierkegaard and Nietzsche and proclaimed that God is dead, attempting to set an atheist point of view within the spectrum of

Christian possibilities. It was a striving for a whole new way of theological understanding. One of the most interesting essays of the movement was Thomas Altizer's 'William Blake and the Role of Myth in the Radical Christian Vision' (1956). There Altizer wrote:

> Ours is a situation that is peculiarly open to the vision of the most radical of all modern Christian visionaries, William Blake, for no poet or seer before him had so profoundly sensed the cataclysmic collapse of the cosmos created by Western man. Yet Blake celebrated this collapse as a way to a total and apocalyptic transfiguration of the world. Can Blake's vision be truly meaningful to us?[13]

Altizer perceived in Blake's poems an anticipation of the metaphysical collapse familiar today to theologians and literary theorists. It is a vision, fluid and evasive, without system – prophetic perhaps, in the prophetic tradition of poetry?

> . . . what Demon
> Hath formed this abominable void,
> This soul-shuddering vacuum? Some said
> 'It is Urizen! But unknown, abstracted,
> Brooding, secret, the dark power hid.

> (*The Book of Urizen* 1: 3–7)

We continue to read great literature. The text survives, and continues to read us. But the reading takes place in a context – a context of belief, a context after Auschwitz, a context of unbelief. Literature does not exist outside value-judgements which are historically variable, even when literature, like Blake, is visionary and prophetic. Our perceptions of literature are not 'objective', nor does literature demand that they should be. Within the rigorous and sceptical demands of contemporary literary theory, literature, not bound by any doctrinal inhibitions, keeps standards in a ruthlessly critical process – a plurisignificant infinite complexity deconstructing the power-structures and the power-relations which both support and destroy our society. A beautiful complexity.

It should be clear that I do feel a great respect for the ruthless logic of Derrida and his programme of deconstruction: an endless interrogation, yet never methodologically independent of the text it interrogates, an ultimate scepticism. Derrida, of course, is well aware that the logic of his exercise cannot be followed *ad infinitum* in the ultimate denial of all truth, meanings and continuity which are, at least relatively, determined and determining.

He is no simple anarchist, or hedonist. But he does pose a fundamental question for theology.

Do we claw our way back towards some kind of notion of linguistic reference, towards metaphysical certainties? Through the freedom of the literary text are we called, in a second naïveté, to a new reconstruction of belief? That is the path of that we have trodden with Paul Ricoeur, anxious to break the autonomy of the verbal icon, to rediscover the complex metaphorical 'encounter with the infinite', to move from the immanence of formalist analysis to the transcendent world the text displays through its sense.

Or do we accept the radical alternative, involving the spiritual freedom and risk of what Don Cupitt (to whose positon I am not subscribing) calls 'the decline of objective theism'? And is this alternative, ultimately perhaps a little familiar to a mystical Christian tradition which is often forgotten, but which somehow returns with its own complexity to the haunted echo-chambers of modern relativism. Cupitt again:

> Here is an anecdote: I have more than once set philosophy of religion students to study *The Ascent of Mount Carmel* and *The Dark Night of the Soul*. 'After all', I say, 'you want to know about God, and St John of the Cross is the best. Admittedly, he is not a philosopher but a mystic. Nevertheless, if man can know God, John did. Let's look at him.' Back come the students, irritable and disappointed: 'There's nothing there,' they complain. 'That's it!', I say, 'That's it!'[14]

This second alternative lies at the heart of the chapter which follows. It is an extended discussion of theodicy, concluding with an examination of one of the novels of Muriel Spark, and leaving us with nothing – or, perhaps, the beginnings of a rediscovery of what Paul Tillich described as the courage to be?

9
Theodicy and Deconstruction

We come finally to a problem central and specific to Christian theology. In brief, how may we sustain a belief in a God of love in the face of evil and the inexplicable and apparently unjustified woes and sufferings imposed on creatures in a world supposedly created and sustained by this beneficent deity? Why do millions of children starve or die of disease; why terrible earthquake; why war and its cruelty? Why are we, in St Paul's words, the slaves of sin? A theodicy might crudely be defined as a writing, doctrine or theory intended, in the Miltonic phrase, to 'justify the ways of God to men' and to uphold a sense of the justice of God before the fact of evil, human waywardness and disobedience. The Judaeo-Christian literary traditions abounds in theodicies, as diverse in form and time as the Book of Job, Milton's *Paradise Lost* (1667), Leibniz's *Theodicy* (1710) or Austin Farrer's *Love Almighty and Ills Unlimited* (1962). Above all, perhaps, the early chapters of Genesis explore our awareness of humanity's radical imperfection, of 'original sin'. It has already been suggested in Chapter 5 (see above p. 113) that this awareness prompts the recognition that a theological criticism should determine the moral relationship between the imperfect reader and the text – a criticism alive not only to human imperfection but also to our innate ability to know and love the truth.

But if we subscribe to such theological determinism, in a manner no doubt ultimatedly attractive to T. S. Eliot, we are left with a literature bound hand and foot by interpretative constraints of highly dubious origins. For, and all too often and uncritically, theology, in practice, works from and towards God as the sole given (see above p. 113). If theology, therefore, itself is a justified enterprise, God holds all the cards, and literature, far from exhibiting any capacity for transformation or indeed justification, is under the dictation of a given which ultimately predetermines what is right and true.

Theodicy, then, would not appear to be a problem. On the other hand, it could be argued that such theology, with its God-givenness, hardly holds out much promise as an enterprise of human discourse. It is inexorably dehumanizing and de-moralizing, its preoccupation with God a denigration of humanity. Furthermore, such preoccupation in human speech makes claims which only God himself can properly make, and theology comes to illustrate and embody 'original sin' as 'an arrogation by man of a relation to God that only God can have to himself.'[1]

In this theological insistence on the givenness of God, therefore, literature is in danger of being bound by precisely those limitations which theodicy seeks to see beyond, and by the illegitimate claim that theology, by its very privileged nature, grants us a critical perspective from which God's love and justice are simply self-evident. Evil, meanwhile, remains a fact and a problem – has, indeed, forced its way into the very core of the argument.

In *proper* theodical discourse, therefore (assuming a theodicy to be a text to which we, as readers or listeners, relate and respond) we need to be clearer as to the point at which we begin, about what we can claim as given at the outset, and about the presuppositions which we bring to our reflections. First, in the Judaeo-Christian tradition, discussion might seem naturally to base itself on a doctrine of the Fall in Eden as the obvious place to begin to think about the justice of God and the problem of sin and evil. In fact, the Fall is an arbitrary place to start one's etiology. For while it may go some way to explain the post-lapsarian condition, it does not explain the Fall itself and the life which preceded it. We are led back, therefore, to a consideration of the creation, the divine plan in creation, and the relationship between divine and humanity creativity.

Second, as I have suggested (see above p. 113), the Western philosphical tradtion has been persistently 'logocentric' and in various ways committed to a belief in some ultimacy of meaning which underlies all language and experience. This ultimate Word lies outside language, directing it and unaffected by linguistic constraints and differences. But are we justified in assuming such extra-linguistic privileges, or upholding the extravangant ontological claims of this Sign or Word? Is it any more helpful or proper to do so than to pursue that kind of theology which has God as its sole given? If such assumptions about theology are destructive for genuine theodicy, equally such logocentricity in the Western tradition is destructive for the language which must constitute theodicy as text. Let us, then, try a radically different theoretical approach which will have bearing upon our thinking about creation, both divine and in human artistry.

Using the thought of Jacques Derrida and the extreme scepticism of deconstruction theory to 'justify the ways of God to man' might seem an odd, not to say foolhardy enterprise. For at the heart of deconstruction is the attempt to reject what, to Derrida, is the fundamental illusion underlying Western metaphysics, that language can be laid aside by reason to 'arrive at a pure, self-authenticating truth or method'.[2] Indeed, after Derrida has dispensed with metaphysics altogether, one of the strengths of his writing is that it is unclassifiable – as philosophy, literature, or even theology. Defying boundaries of academic discourse, it presents a challenge to text or any linguistic construct, and perhaps, therefore, may be of profit in unbinding those theodicies which find themselves to be texts hampered by the claims of theology or the need to provide answers to a problem.

We have seen how structuralist theory, derived in the first instance from the linguistics of Saussure, asserts the purely arbitrary connection between the sign and its material object. Deconstruction goes even further, denying that any meaning is immediately present in a sign. A sign or word is defined as much by what it does *not* mean as by what it does mean, so that meaning is as much absent as present. Meaning can never be nailed down, can never be quite grasped, is always, in a sense *deferred*.

Language then, is viewed as a *differential* structure of meaning, which is derived only from the differences between words, and from what makes them distinct. 'Dog' and 'log' are distinguished by the difference in their initial consonant, and as we begin to distinguish between them, a structure of meaning slowly begins to emerge, and the sense of language becomes dependent on a structure of differences. Structuralism goes this far. Where Derrida and deconstruction go beyond the structuralist enterprise is in the desire to shed all vestiges of the Western metaphysical tradition – that 'logocentricity' which still lurks in structuralism. The advantage of such full-blooded relativism it might seem, is that one can dispense with all belief systems and sit loose to the claims of religious doctrine. But is this just an ultimate exercise in passing the buck and refusing all responsibility? With deconstruction, it would seem, literature simply exhibits its own failure in referentiality, an exercise in indecision *ad infinitum*. Or, the question has been asked in another, highly significant way, recalling the language of Philippians 2:7.

> Is it just that now, in a religious twist to the old ideology, victory is achieved by *kenosis* or self-emptying; the winner is the one who has managed to get rid of all his cards and sit with empty hands.[3]

The winner, we might say, is the one who 'made himself nothing, assuming the nature of a slave'. The point is now to establish the value for our discussion of deconstruction's radical purifying strategy – a positive value for theology and theodicy.

In Chapter 2 of *Of Grammatology*, entitled 'Linguistics and Grammatology', Derrida takes Saussure to task in his promotion of *speech* and relegation of *writing* to a secondary status. It is time now to explore this a little further. Speech, in Saussure and according to Derrida, is self-conscious, the occasion of experiencing 'meaning' in the link between sound and sense, ultimately proclaiming the priority of concept over language. This priority of speech has produced 'the system of language associated with phonetic-alphabetic writing [which] is that within which logocentric metaphysics, determining the sense of being as presence, has been produced'.[4] Derrida avoids such adhesion to a metaphysical tradition by granting a priority to *writing* as a precondition of speech – writing not merely as a graphical exercise but as 'archi-écriture', the 'free-play' of difference within language structures, a depersonalized medium, free and independent of the powerful self-defining and conceptualizing tendencies of uttered speech.

Although deconstruction adheres extremely closely to the text it is considering, it is very far from celebrating the prestige of the written text of Western literature, philosophy and theology. Rather, in his reading of Saussure, Derrida is not denying the whole Saussurian project, but demonstrating that a radical driving of the text to its final conclusions will banish conceptual presuppositions upon which, presumably, the language is balanced. Derrida objects to that

Logocentricism which, limiting the internal system of language in general by a bad abstraction, prevents Saussure and the majority of his successors from determining fully and explicitly that which is called 'the integral and concrete object of linguistics'. But conversely . . . it is when he is not expressly dealing with writing, when he feels he has closed the parentheses on that subject, that Saussure opens the field of a general grammatology.

. . . Then something which was never spoken of and which is nothing other than writing itself as the origin of language writes itself within Saussure's discourse.

(*Of Grammatology*, pp. 43–4)

We discover, therefore, in the text itself a perpetual denial both of meaning and also the pronouncement of conclusions which rest ultimately upon some extralinguistic concept or signifier. Rather we come to recognize writing as a never-ending displacement and deferral, escaping the delusions of a stable and self-deceiving tradition. There are no answers, only extreme scepticism, and a continual evasion of the self-enclosed systematizing of texts by which we long to find meaning – the answer to our problem, the final solution.

This is the chilly alternative offered by deconstruction. By a ruthlessly literal reading of texts it demonstrates how they ultimately deny their own logic and confess what they deny. Writing, not merely secondary and derivative, actually exposes the condition of all discourse, that it can neither say precisely what it means, nor in honesty, mean what it says. With its battle-cry *Il n'y a pas de hors-texte* ('There is nothing outside the text'), deconstuction may indeed be subversive, but it is so with a devastating honesty which refuses to be conned by order, dogma or conclusion which it is claimed is supported by the text but for which the text itself can provide no grounding. The text therefore will always defy the system which claims to give it order. A term frequently used by Derrida, and his American disciple Paul de Man, is *aporia*, meaning a paradox created from within, which thinking encounters and beyond which thought is helpless. As Christopher Norris puts it, 'what deconstuction persistently reveals is an ultimate impasse of thought engendered by a rhetoric that always insinuates its own textual workings into the truth claims of philosophy'.[5]

As we return then, to the classical problem of theodicy – how we can believe in a good God in a world so full of evil – let us allow *writing*, in the Derridaan sense, its head unrepressed by philosophy or by the demands of theological system. Let us deliberately engage in an act of literary *kenosis* in obedience to an honesty which may well entail a death but may also be a redemption.

II

Is it right to begin our reflections on theodicy at a specific metaphysical starting-point, an original point of pure creation in Eden which establishes a paradigm of goodness from which mankind falls (the problem of evil) and to which we struggle to return (to the undivided splendour of God's glory)? After all, in the *very* beginning of creation, before God started pronouncing things as good, the earth was without form or void – nothing, without any prior claim aesthetic or moral. Let us then see the dangers in the attempt of one modern theologian (and one with unusual literary sensitivity) to lay a foundation for theodicy – Austin Farrer in *Love Almighty and Ills Unlimited* (1962)

In his discussion of the workings of God in our apparently disordered world, Farrer draws a familiar analogy between the divine act of creation and the human act of artistic or literary creativity. He asserts that 'the process of artistic invention probably casts as much light as anything human on God's devising of the world'.[6] The human analogy is, he admits, limited, but still useful. It allows us to say something of the glory of sheer inventiveness, the beauty of order, even the mysterious processes of origination in the ability to make both excellent and new whatever is made. But, Farrer further admits, it is limited because it casts no light on God's prefering creation to another. The particular creativity of the artist may be perceived in terms of previous personal history or situation, or *as artist* he may be admitted to have no existence or actuality outside the artifact.[7] God's 'prior actuality' before his creation is different from that of the human artist, according to Farrer. For no situation confronted God before the world was, but nor is Farrer prepared to abandon God's actuality or intentions in the face of the independence of the artifact of his creating; is not prepared, in the end, to abandon the scholastic absoluteness of the Supreme Being and Creator at the heart of his theodicy.

In his lecture, 'The Prior Actuality of God' (1966), Farrer inclines towards an image of the action of God in creation in an analogy with a hypothetical playwright who 'is not condemned to confine his active existence within the production of plays. Quite apart from, and prior to, his activity as producer-playwright, he has a personal life of his own . . . his *prior actuality* in respect of the play is not simply his initiative in creating it but his life exterior to it; a life out of which flows his creation of it' (*Reflective Faith*, p. 180). For theodicy, of course, this life exterior to creation is a vital security to the belief that the creation was God's intention and that, in spite of all, his intentions were that it be good ('And God saw all that he had made, and it was very good'.) His intentions, in other words, are entirely successfully effected in his work and ultimately, if the theodicy is to be sustained, nothing lies outside God's beneficence and omnipotence.

The key difficulty in the analogy between the creator God and the human artist lies in what has already been mentioned frequently in this book, the problem of *intentional fallacy* – the argument that the design or intention of an author, for example, is neither available nor desirable as a standard for judging a work of literary art. Given this disjunction in human creativity, between intention and effect, on what literary basis are we to grant to the divine author a privilege not available to the human – that he effects in creation exactly what he intends? I speak deliberately of a 'literary basis'. For this privilege theological orthodoxy, in speaking of creativity, would enlist such heavy-weight arguments as the perfection and omnicompetence of God in contrast to human frailty and imperfection. But in the realm of theodicy we are also necessarily in the realm of textuality and in defending the goodness of God in the face of evil, theodicy becomes text, that is a literary structure and therefore subject to literary conditions. Theodical reflection, therefore, as an interpretation of a great mystery is bound by the limits of textuality and literary criticism which is also itself an interpretation – so that in theodicy there is, unavoidably, no necessary connection between intention and effect. Does, then, this textual nature of theodicy pose an insuper-able problem for theology, suggesting that there is no satisfactory means of justifying the ways of God to men, evil either remaining a mystery or a theodicy inevitably promulgating 'a downright horrible conception of God', as William Empson claims of Milton in his book *Milton's God* (1961)? Or, on the other hand, is this very textuality a way of releasing us from the false assumptions and presuppositions of a theological absolutism out of which we may deconstruct our sense of the divine workings into a new sense of freedom and a new discernment of the mystery?

Underlying Austin Farrer's theodicy is his response to Leibniz's work *Theodicy: Essays on the Goodness of God, the Freedom of Man, and the Origin of Evil* (1710), which he edited and to which he wrote an Introduction in 1951. Leibniz tends to approach the problem of evil as an intellectual puzzle rather than as an actual threat to the meaning of life.[8] He postulates the indispensability of evil in a creation of the maximum variety and possibility, writing that

> The wisdom of God, not content with embracing all the possi-
> bilities, penetrates them, compares them, weighs them one
> against the other, to estimate their degrees of perfection or
> imperfection, the strong and the weak, the good and the evil.
> It goes even beyond the finite combinations, it makes of them
> an infinity of infinites, that is to say, an infinity of possible
> sequences of the universe, each of which contains an infinity of
> creatures. By this means the divine Wisdom distributes all the
> possibles it had already contemplated separately, into so many
> universal systems which it further compares the one with the
> other. The result of all these comparisons and deliberations is
> the choice of the best from among all these possible systems,
> which wisdom makes in order to satisfy goodness completely;
> and such is precisely the plan of the universe as it is.[9]

In short, according to Leibniz, 'all the evils of the world contribute, in ways which generally we cannot now trace, to the character of the whole as the best of all possible universes' (para. 9).

Farrer, it is true, is not a reliable or accurate observer of Leibniz. There is far more to the subtlety and the 'infinite possibilities' of the *Theodicy* than Farrer is prepared to admit. But his response is in the broad tradition of eighteenth century interpreters from Voltaire to Hume which found Leibniz deterministic, cruel and morally offensive. Farrer as a Christian believer suggests that there is a danger in making God incarnate into a 'solution' to the problem of theodicy, Christ a mere philosopher and the mystery of divine revelation therefore unnecessary.

Leibniz . . . writes with perfect seriousness and decency about the Christian scheme of redemption, but it hardly looks like being for him a crucial deliverance from perdition. It is not the intervention of Mercy, by which alone He possesses himself of us: it is 'one of the ways in which supreme benevolence carries out a cosmic policy; and God's benevolence is known by pure reason, and apart from Christian revelation.[10]

If scholars of Leibniz criticize Farrer's crudifying of the *Theodicy*, Voltaire it is generally recognized, despite his bitter criticisms of so-called 'optimistic' theodicy with its confidence in this best of all possible worlds, probably had never even read Leibniz at first hand. He was responding to what was in the air of eighteenth century thought.

Farrer and Voltaire on Leibniz illustrate very clearly the disjunction between the 'intention' behind a work and its 'effect'. The *Theodicy* prompted an anger in Voltaire far removed from Leibniz himself. It was the stark fact of the Lisbon earthquake disaster of 1755 which led Voltaire to repudiate as inadequate the apparently insensitive complacency of philosophers who preached to the people that all was for the best, implying merely divine indifference and callousness. Their cruelty is ironically described in the Preface to the *Poem on the Disaster of Lisbon* (1756).

The heirs of the dead would now come into their fortunes, masons would grow rich in rebuilding the city, beasts would grow fat on corpses buried in the ruins; such is the natural effect of natural causes. So don't worry about your own particular evil; you are contributing to the general good.'[11]

But it is in *Candide* (1758), that Voltaire mocks most tellingly the perversions to which Leibnizian 'optimism' and its version of Christian othodoxy is liable, portrayed in the character of the windbag philosopher Pangloss. In the end Leibniz's speculations about the intentions of God in creating a world of human experience merely stifle human initiative and the ability of human beings to help one another. Pangloss remarks to Candide:

There is a chain of events in this best of all possible worlds; for if you had not been turned out of a beautiful mansion at the point of a jackboot for the love of Lady Cunegarde, and if you had not been involved in the Inquisition, and had not wandered

over America on foot, and had not struck the Baron with your
sword, and lost all those sheep you brought from Eldorado, you
would not be here eating candied fruit and pistachio nuts.

(Penguin edn, p. 144)

The only possible response to such a deterministic narrative of
cause and effect, and to further attempts to find a solution to the
problem of evil, is work without reasoning in the garden and
silence.[12] In *Candide*, Voltaire responds to the moral cruelty which
he sees implied in Leibnizian theodicy with the elusive freedom,
the humour and irony, the endless pluralities and impenetrability
of literary and textual device.[13] Within these dynamics are recast
at least the proper bases for theodicy in a serious respect for
human freedom, compassion in the face of inexplicable woe, and
a preservation of the sense of the human which is too often pre-
empted by institutions and by theoretical presuppositions.

David Hume, too, in his *Dialogues Concerning Natural Religion*
(1779), employed literary devices to criticize Leibnizian theology.
By the form of the dialogue, Hume preserves a freedom of shifting
perspective, a dramatic balance that refuses to fall into dogmatism
and protects Hume himself from identification with some precon-
ceived position. The potential determinism of the Leibniziam
universe is avoided in the irony, humour, and multiple perspectives of the dialogues.

Finally, in the eighteenth century, Immanuel Kant, whom I
have already linked with the critical tradition which culminates
in deconstruction, was deeply affected by Leibniz and seriously
concerned with the establishment of an authentic theodicy.
Rejecting the ontological argument for the existence of God, and
in his dispassionate study of the natural order, it might appear
that for Kant reference to the deity would tend simply to become
redundant. That it did not was due, in Austin Farrer's opinion, to
'illusions of projections' and 'contextual encouragements'[14] in the
field of human action which, for Farrer, are never substantial
enough to bear the full load of religious belief. Against Leibniz,
Kant certainly did not believe that human beings were capable of
direct description and comment on the person of God in his
creative activity. Dispensing with a speculative theology which
would seek to link its images intrinsically with temporal concepts
and perceptions, Kant did not deny the value of theological
language as analogy and as an attempt to relate the world of

senses, by recognition and reaction, to that which is beyond its perimeter; to recognize it, in Kant's words 'for what it is for me, namely in respect of the world of which I am a part'.[15]

Kant, Voltaire and Hume responded to Leibniz's *Theodicy* primarily in a literary mode. But each, at the same time, either rejected or made impossibly difficult the language of theism and denied proper theological discourse. In the case of Kant, the question must be raised as to whether the analogical symbols of theological language properly do express our relationship with that of which we have intrinsically no direct apprehension, Kant being so unwilling to invest his talk of the divine with the substance of religious conviction. Indeed this aspect of Kant brings to mind T. E. Hulme's definition of prose as 'a museum of metaphor', his attempted theological utterance a self-contained system which no longer needs God, a signifier that has lost its signification.[16]

But might this seemingly negative conclusion be seen in another light, as freeing theological discourse from the perennial problem of its primordial given? These inter-texts of Leibniz, for which Leibniz's *Theodicy* itself, it may be, was no more than a necessary *pre-text*, on a literary basis begin to reassemble the priorities in creation and to propose a new basis for theodicy. What, then, of Farrer's *Love Almighty and Ills Unlimited* in this company? It has already been suggested that Farrer's analogy between the creator God and the human artist involves a problem of intentionality – that though we may wish to assume that God effectively creates precisely what he intends to, the textuality of theodical discourse necessarily throws up from that assumption a ghastly, Empsonian image of the Almighty. For in *all* textuality, there is a fracture between intention and effect. But it will be recalled also that Farrer does admit that the analogy is an imperfect one, on the basis of God's greater freedom to prefer one possible creation to another. God's goodness and creativity are seen in terms of an inexhaustible inventiveness – his omipotence lies in his freedom to choose what to invent, 'an element of sheer inventiveness which is his supreme glory' (*Love Almighty*, pp. 62–3). This godlike power is transmitted to God's creatures, whose freedom from predetermination is also a freedom of choice (significantly limited) which, it might be proposed shifts from God the blame for the evils they experience.

But in our pursuit of an authentic theodicy we have gone too far, too fast. Let us return to the notion of God's inexhaustible inventiveness, a return in Farrer (aligning him with Voltaire,

Hume and Kant) to an enacted elusiveness, a shifting of attention
in theodicy, in Roland Barthes' terms, from *l'oeuvre* to *l'écriture*
(see above p.107). God's creativity is now perceived not in terms
of its object, the effect achieved, but in terms of enactment no
longer limited by the completed work 'which oversees, controls,
purifies, banalizes, codifies, corrects, imposes . . .' (Barthes). That
is when theodicy becomes a system demanding a solution.

Instead, what do we have? Insofar as a theodicy must be seen
as a text, or rather textuality as the vehicle for theodicy, an attempt
to reflect in organized language the theodical problem of evil
experienced in the creation of a *good God*, we have slipped into a
realm of shifting relativities, the 'deconstruction' of dogmatic or
metaphysical contamination of perfect freedom and endless,
glorious inventiveness. The text is now freed to embarrass its own
ruling system of logic,[17] reading perceives the *aporia* in the text,
the qualities of self-contradiction. In effect, any sense of meaning
is now ultimately deferred, literary disjunction between creative
intention and effect placed within the context of an endlessly
repeated interpretative act, delight experienced in the rich creative
act and the demand for a solution finally deferred, as is quite right,
to the ultimacy and infinitude of God's good time.

The defence rests in openness and plenitude. A theodicy, as
text, enacts the multiplicity of divine creation – the text outman-
oeuvering the threatening limits of its own logic, text calling to
text (Leibniz to Voltaire to Farrer) in a play of intertextuality in
which particulars combine in an interplay which joyfully trans-
gresses all limits and rules. By a radical process of defamiliarization
no theory is allowed to dominate and grow stale in a perpetual
realignment of elements in the story. Farrer, though he would
hardly have rejoiced in the actual writings of Derrida, saw the
point in his chapter on 'Adam and Lucifer'.

What is the use of raking up these old-world stories? Because,
however dead in theory, they are alive in our emotions. When
the spiritually-minded or the tender-hearted nowadays
complain that nature is too bad to be natural, and that the
physical order is fallen, what makes them think so? Or by what
standard of the ought-to-be do they condemn the things that
are? My sympathy supports the lament, but my reason derides
it. For I do not believe any of the propositions required to give
it substance. I do not believe the purposiveness of natural

agents, the hierarchy of causes, or the inertness of matter. I
think that God's creation begins from below with a chaos of non-
rational forces, each acting of itself with inexhaustible energy.

(Love Almighty, pp. 146–7)

The story of Eden and the figure of Satan remain alive in our
emotions, and in the textuality of theodicy they continue to
address the problem of suffering and evil in God's world, however
dead their 'theory'. Creation begins 'from below' in a confusion
of inexhaustible energy.

Recent criticism of *Paradise Lost* has recognized the characteristics
of theodical texts. Stanley Fish in his book *Surprised by Sin* (1967)
begins by acknowledging the power of Satan's first great speech
(*Paradise Lost*, I, 84–124), with its defiance indicative of splendid
courage, qualities of leadership and endurance. The reader,
indeed, is almost seduced into a feeling of sympathy with Satan
against a distinctly self-satisfied deity.

> We may with more successful hope resolve
> To wage by force or guile eternal war
> Irreconcilable to our grand Foe
> Who now triumphs, and in th' excess of joy
> Sole reigning holds the tyranny of heav'n.

But if the reader's immediate reaction to Satan is a degree of
admiration, Milton immediately complicates this response with
the more disparaging line –

> So spake th' apostate Angel, though in pain,
> Vaunting aloud, but racked with deep despair.

> (125–6)

Things are not what they seem. Milton's Satan has prompted a
certain sympathetic response from the reader, which authorial
comment immediately, it might almost be said, falsifies. In Fish's
words, 'there is a disparity between our response to the speech
and the epic voice's evaluation of it.'[18]

Fish acknowledges intention on the part of Milton, but perceives
the process of meaning as taking place within the reader. Alive in
our emotions, the text unsettles us to live in a drama (between

reader and poem), in which we become, like Adam, responsible within the overarching context of textual control. The reader tends to construct the text in the face of the repeated insidious attack of verbal power.

Milton, we may say, was a great poet. May we take up Farrer's analogy and suggest that God is, indeed, the true artist, drawing his creation into a freedom of response, yet authoritative, never meaning quite what he says or saying quite what he means in an infinite deferment of meaning which is crucial to theodical reflection? Such reflection will surely entail a sceptical refusal to become preoccupied with the primordial 'given' of theology, that is God himself. For, as Ray L. Hart has pointed out 'Such theology, both in principle and in performance, is a dehumanizing and a detemporalizing enterprise. Its derogation of humanity is achieved precisely by means of preoccupation with *God*. In fact, it *illustrates* 'original sin' through its preoccupation with God in the way that only God can be preoccupied with himself.'[19] Such theological fabrication of a given is an enactment of that which theodicy abhors, and the very textuality of theodical discourse, as we have described it, will tend towards its deconstruction. God, the true artist, slips away behind his work.

What Professor Hart describes as the 'active symbolic imagination' (p. 243)[20] has, as its first task, the avoidance of its own ossification, its tendency to deteriorate into lifeless formulae and theories, which William Lynch calls the 'exploiting appendages' of theology.[21] The concern of the imagination is not, in the first instance, ontological, but, in art, the control of perspective in such a way as to invite *perception* (Coleridge's word in *Biographia Literaria*) and prompt a tendency. So it is with God, the great artist, and human freedom. Hart draws the analogy between the problem of the communication of a work of art and the problem of the communication of revelation: 'but can only presuppose among the communicants a world of delineated things and a jaded sensibility' (p. 248).

True perception, the ability really to look at things, is a great destroyer of idols, and the textuality of proper theodical discourse will deconstructively lead us beyond a myopic concern with the limited conclusions drawn from a closure of the text, to a teleological perspective, a faithful *commitment* to deferment of meaning and image. Farrer in his theodicy perceived this clearly. The poet is one who sees and contemplates most profoundly (see above p.35), creative in the perception of things in abandoned love even to the point of their created mystery. Enactment is all. And so to begin to recognize something of the mystery of divine creativity in a perplexing world, we need to pass beyond the fictions of finite human understanding into greater honesty, a greater commitment of faith.

Utter perversity – utter honesty, of the reading process. The text obsessively illustrating its own insufficiency and challenging the reader in his equally obsessive desire to set up the 'verbal icon' – a timeless, self-possessed structure of meaning. Verbal power at pains to deny what it seems repeatedly to invite – an answer to the problem of its meaning. And outside the text there is, of course, nothing.

It is then, finally, a question of all or nothing. There are no vain, comforting consolations. Farrer gives an example of such a 'consolation'. 'Don't you know about young Harry? He hurt his spine and kept his bed eighteen months, just at the age when boys grow strong and daring. But it all turned out for the best, it made him so much more thoughtful than other lads . . . these trials are sent to teach us'. (*Love Almighty*. p. 166). But in such an instance when good ends are claimed to emerge from evil, the evil will continue to breed after its own kind. For Farrer the issue is all or nothing; either we believe or we do not (p. 169). The evil fact of young Harry's damaged spine is evil and that is all there is to it. It cannot be explained away by any instrumental view of evil. I want to deny, against Schleiermacher and what John Hick calls the 'Irenaean Type of Theodicy', that evil actually will serve the good purpose of God. But such a denial and such belief is a great daring, an ultimate scepticism of system, a repression, by theology or culture, of any dangerous knowledge of its own constitution.

Theodical textuality, endlessly deconstructive of its own conclusions, is but a mirror or looking glass reflecting back to us with ruthless honesty. And, Farrer asserts, when we pray, 'the hand of God does somewhat put aside that accursed looking glass, which each of us holds before him, and which shows each of us our own face. Only the day of judgement will strike the glass for ever from our hands, and leave us nowhere reflected but in the pupils of the eyes of God'.[22] The metaphysical denial of deconstructive procedures is not (certainly in Derrida himself) a denial of the existence of anything but discourse, or the affirmation of pure difference. But it may be that the purifying process of deferment until the day of judgement is a denial of a metaphysical lodging for evil in a pure form – a scepticism which finally rests only in the purity of a good at a point insufficiently striven for by language, beyond all reach. 'And God saw all that he had made, and it was (in God's eyes) very good.'

III

In 1984, Muriel Spark published a novel with the title *The Only Problem*. It is about a man, Harvey Gotham, who is writing a monograph on the Book of Job.

> For he could not face that a benevolent Creator, one whose charming and delicious light descended and spread over the world, and being powerful everywhere, could condone the unspeakable sufferings of the world; that God did permit all suffering and was therefore by logic of his omnipotence, the actual author of it, he was at a loss how to square with the existence of God, given the premise that God is good.
>   'It is the only problem', Harvey had always said. Now, Harvey believed in God, and this was what tormented him. 'It's the only problem, in fact, worth discussing'
>
> (Triad. ed. p. 19)

Harvey spends a great deal of time discussing this problem. He talks about it at great length, while around him extraordinary events are taking place.

Immensely rich and living in seclusion in France, Harvey is told that his estranged wife Effie is suspected of terrorist activities which eventually result in the death of a Paris policeman. Though it is never proved conclusively (was Effie instead the girl photographed in a mountain commune in California?), Harvey is repeatedly questioned by the police and hounded by the press. To everyone, his preferred topic of conversation is the Book of Job – the only problem after all. Comforters descend chaotically upon him, in the shape of Ruth, the wife of his best friend, with the infant Clara, Effie's child by another man; his lawyer, Stewart Cowper – a self-confessed comforter (p. 121); the puritanical Aunt Pet. Harvey remains curiously unmoved, absorbed in his problem and a frequent visitor to the nearby *Musée* of Epinal to contemplate Georges De La Tour's painting *Job Visited by His Wife*. The biblical record of the sayings of Job's wife is brief and apparently uncomplimentary: 'Then his wife said to him, "Are you still unshaken in your integrity? Curse God and die!" ' (Job 2:9). Yet to Harvey, this violent, impatient woman is seen in De La Tour's painting as a loving, solicitous wife, looking with compassion on her suffering husband.[23] What does this ambiguous text (Jerome translates her words as *benedic Deo*, knowing that the Hebrew *bless* is, in fact, a euphemism for its exact opposite, *curse*. But does bless really mean bless here?) and this ambiguous painting *mean*? Whatever her words, Job's wife seems tender and loving to Harvey, an idealisation of the painter; 'in his dream, Job and his wife are deeply in love' (p. 78).

Is this problem of suffering actually that we are never prepared to face it except as a problem to be solved? What, for example, of God in Harvey's study of the Book of Job? Harvey admits that he approaches the only problem by analyzing the God of Job (p. 180), avoiding self-analysis, for it is God who asks the questions in Job's book. God must, therefore, provide the answers. But it is clear that God as a character comes out very badly (p. 30), so much so indeed, that the reporters entirely miss the point of Harvey's discussion of Job and imagine that he is *condemning* God (as a literary critic one is reminded of Empson). '*God is a Shit* was one of the blasphemies preached at an international press conference held yesterday . . .' (p. 123).

The difficulty, as Harvey knows full well, is that in discussing the Book of Job we construct a character called God. He denies hotly the press accusations.

> . . . you've got to understand that I said nothing whatsoever about God. I mean our Creator. What I was talking about was a fictional character in the Book of Job, called God.
>
> (p. 135)

It is from this fictional character that theodical judgement tends to be made. This character asks the questions, and is perceived to cause Job unmerited sufferings (p. 109). He provides, perhaps, a context for the problem, but to suggest that he provides the answer results in an enormity – the conclusion that God is simply a Shit.

The fictional character of God in Job tends to direct the

discussion along the lines of a *moral* argument. That is, following the conclusions of the Comforters, if you suffer it must mean that you have done something to deserve it. It is a question of moral cause and effect. If that be the case, then God, as arbiter of morality, is indeed abhorrent. As Harvey says, 'But Job made the point that he didn't deserve it. Suffering is'nt in proportion to what the sufferer deserves' (p. 50). He goes on to suggest that the cause of suffering may be actually our limitations of knowledge (p. 111). That, in our inadequate way, we try to suggest solutions to the problem which might seem to make some sense – the neat solution that suffering is earned by bad behaviour. But suffering is thereby simply compounded, created, by the very limitations of the theories which try to explain its mystery. We construct a fictional character – God; we construct moral solutions; and our constructions bring about suffering – the righteous indignation of Job.

Throughout *The Only Problem* we come closest to the demonic in the rigidity of conventions, untruth dangerously evident in the lack of subtlety of quick conclusions and neat accusations. At one point Harvey suggest that Job's initial difficulties arise from the fact that he was too conventional, 'so much so that God was bored with him' (p. 149). In making their case against Effie, the French police carefully orchestrate their control of public opinion so as not to confuse the issue.

> 'I think you should publish the police-photo from Trieste,' said Harvey. 'To be perfectly fair. They are both Effie. The public might not then be prejudiced.'
>   'Oh, the public is not so subtle as to make these nice distinctions'.
>
>   (p. 163)

Justice it seems, is carried out on a very limited budget, intended to make things clear and simple, but actually a limitation which lies very close to the heart of suffering itself.

For conventional behaviour with its accommodations to public limitation simply fails to reckon with – and therefore tends to contribute to – the *necessity* of suffering in human life. Harvey recognizes this need, 'to study, to think, is to live and suffer painfully' (p. 153), and knows how becalmed life would be without suffering. The problem in the end for Harvey, perhaps, is he is over-protected (p. 64), unable to deal with the problem of suffering because everyone conspires, like Job's comforters, to estrange him from it. And that, it may be, *is* the only problem. Harvey objects strongly to scholars who try to rearrange the verses of the Book of Job so as to make sense where there is obviously no sense. Such rationalization entirely misses the point and actually creates a problem. For the Book of Job will never come clear. Furthermore, as Harvey says, 'It does'nt matter; it's a poem' (p. 132). Just as Job himself upsets all the theology of his friends (p. 52), so the Book upsets all reason, resists conclusions, and by evading easy answers to the question of theodicy, does not evade the stark fact of suffering. In the same way, Harvey objects to modern, 'clear' translations of the Bible. 'They all try to reach everybody and end by saying nothing to anybody' (p. 133).[24] Living with suffering, in obscurity and ambiguity, prepared to accept discontinuity, admitting one's confusion before God like Job (Job 42:1–6), is perhaps the answer to the only problem, though not an explanation.

Harvey finishes his monograph on the Book of Job. It is not quite clear what has happened to his first family, his wife Effie. But, like Job, he is rewarded with a new family, miscellaneously assembled. What is there left to do? 'Live another hundred and forty years. I'll have three daughters, Clara, Jemima and Eye Paint' (p. 189). Hardly conventional! Facing the only real problem, Harvey's 'solution' seems no solution in the world's eyes, its substance even invisible. And for this, actually, his friends envy him. '[Edward] . . . felt envious of Harvey for his invisible and probably non-existent girl and her baby' (p. 33).

No God: no theory. Yet Job, and Harvey, are somehow restored. The process has been one of deconstruction, undermining all strategies and every presence. Undermining the logic of God's omnipotence, the logic of the text. This movement away from rationalistic attempts to 'prove' the goodness of God, or to structure and delimit the experience of evil, in endless deferment, is a movement towards the rediscovery of faith. Half-persuaded by the quite competent theologising of Job's Comforters, we are jolted unexpectedly and unreasonably by the Book's conclusion justifying Job's baffled arguing from the depths of his misery.

The respect is literary – a final respect for the textuality of theodicy (a kind of respect we actually very rarely grant to Scripture). There are no answers but a brave and honest faith, in we know not what, and in spite of all.[25]

10

Conclusion

In the course of this book I have referred, in varying degrees of detail, to four essays all bearing the title 'Religion and Literature'. Their authors are T. S. Eliot, Cleanth Brooks, David Hesla and John J. McDonald. I began with Eliot and with him I will finish.

Cleanth Brooks, writing in the *Sewanee Review* in 1974, is anxious to make a clear distinction between the functions of literature and religion. It might seem an obvious point, but it cannot be made too often since, in fact, the two are often confused. In particular, if it is right that it was the 'failure' of religion in the nineteenth century which led to the growth of English studies, there has been a corresponding tendency to replace religion with literature. Brooks develops his point, suggesting that a religion makes some ultimate claims on us and demands a commitment. A literary experience on the other hand does not. Nevertheless, religion and literature, or more specifically for Brooks, poetry, need one another, and for many reasons. Not least, poetry needs religion 'to carry on certain funcitons with which poetry might be tempted to encumber itself'. But happy is the man who possesses both 'religion and poetry, faith and imagination, the one complementing the other, neither cramped and misshapen through being forced to substitute for something other than itself'.[1]

I both applaud and deplore Cleanth Brooks' arguments. He is surely right in his anxiety to keep literature and religion apart, and not to allow their overlap to develop into a merger. Poetry and imaginative literature is not a short cut to religious truth, a sugaring of the theological pill for those who are not prepared to look carefully and with hard thinking into the nature of divine mysteries. Equally, 'religious' people neglect the insights and beauty of poetry and the art of literature at their peril. Wordsworth put one point of view of the distinction and affinity between religion and poetry.

. . . between religion – making up the deficiencies of reason by faith; and poetry – passionate for the instruction of reason: between religion – whose element is infinitude and whose ultimate trust is the supreme of things, submitting herself to circumscription and reconciled to substitutions; and poetry – ethereal and transcendent, yet incapable to sustain her existence without sensuous incarnation.[2]

Nevertheless, I am extremely uneasy about Brooks' sense of 'religion' which he sees as little more than the profoundest element in 'the fundamental human situation' (p. 102). Having made that assertion, without further definiton, he then implies that the *functions* of religion involve certain encumbrances – commitment to a 'fixed creed', for example – which are at variance with that fundamental 'precious freedom' so dear to poetry and literature.

There is a muddle here which I perceive also, though to a lesser degree, in David Hesla's essay in the *Journal of the American Academy of Religion*. Hesla wants to avoid discussions of 'literature and theology' or 'literature and Christianity'. He desires rather to be as free as possible to examine the 'religious dimensions' of literature, and to turn his attention to 'the analysis of the religious significance of popular culture'.[3] Hesla, quite rightly, does not wish to be bound to the traditions of Western philosophy and theology. But it seems to me that his approach, like that of Brooks, is in danger of diluting 'religion' to a point where, as the plaything of sociologists, cultural anthropologists, literary critics and many others, it simply becomes vacuous and theologically trivial. While on the other hand, though it does in some way demand a commitment, religion must avoid at all costs the 'demands of apologetic theology' (Hesla), and is almost at pains to deny to the Christian West two thousand years of serious theology and spirituality.

Agreeing with Brooks, therefore, concerning the 'polar relationship' between literature and religion, I wish also to recover a sense of the *theological* importance of the enterprise, and not in the sense that this necessarily implies that kind of intellectualism which correlates religious faith with mere assent to a body of propositions, or the loss of freedom.

Indeed, I find this sense of freedom to be central to our whole enterprise. In my initial discussion of Eliot's essay 'Religion and Literature', I suggested that he is there proposing a paradoxical and uneasy relationship between two substantive categories (see above, p. 8). John McDonald, in his essay, written to inaugurate the journal *Religion and Literature* in 1984, professes that his purpose is to 'try fully to destabilize that paradox – to make it living and uncertain and contingent but fertile, organized, and natural'.[4] The continuous interplay between religion or theology and literature should ensure that 'no hierarchy of terms is sacred or privileged beyond question', that we remain open to the risks, excitements and contingencies of the struggle for truth which, as McDonald observes, is the only truth we certainly possess.

In the end however, and despite all that I have said, indeed, the burden of my writing is, that, following Eliot, the 'greatness' of literature cannot be determined solely by literary standards. I believe with both Plato and Aristotle that, even though we may wish to abandon Eliot's 'explicit ethical and theological standards', poetry must be shown to be of serious ethical benefit and it can be only properly understood *sub specie aeternitatis*. I have mentioned more than once the Aristotelian mimetic theory which argues that literature does not merely imitate or copy, but completes and fulfills nature. Or it imitates an action which is never in nature so fully realized. In this literary tradition of mimesis, Eliot suggested that 'it is not enough to understand what we ought to be, unless we know what we are; and we do not understand what we are, unless we know what we ought to be' (see above. p. 9) In literature we glimpse, at times, the fulfilment of our nature, cast in the imaginative genius of great art, and continuing to persuade us of the value and ultimate truth of the theological enterprise as a seeking for utterance of the divine mystery as it is known and felt in our experience.

I do not expect an even response to what I have said in the preceding pages. My meditations and arguments have wandered far in a short space, and in many modes. I have been aware of allowing different moods to direct my writing, and I have been aware that sometimes I am quite clear about my purposes, while at others I have struggled with what I feel to be important, but perceive very imperfectly and with limited understanding. At least I hope I have been honest. This sense of the provisional, and of the possible, the sense of contradiction or, in better moments, of vitality, seems to me to be proper for anyone who is concerned with theology as a living enterprise. We need continually to be reminded that we undertake our task in the context of a journey and of change: but it is creative change, and it is above all the poet in his process of invention who illuminates for us the nature of God's mysterious creative redemptive activity. Must we, then, for God's sake, forever take leave of the God of our poor theologizing and faint spirituality, setting out on our theological journeys afresh, abandoning the old referents, signifiers that have lost their signification? Perhaps. 'For now see through a glass, darkly, but then face to face; now I know in part: but then I shall know even as also I am known.'

Notes

CHAPTER 1: INTRODUCTION

1. Giles Gunn, *The Interpretation of Otherness, Literature, Religion, and the American Imagination* (New York, 1979) p.5.
2. Ziolkowski, *Fictional Transfigurations of Jesus* (Princeton, 1972) p.229.
3. Mark C. Taylor (ed.), *Deconstruction in Context: Literature and Philosophy*, (Chicago and London, 1986) pp.33–4.
4. Merleau-Ponty, *The Visible and the Invisible* (1968) in Taylor, op. cit. p.321.
5. Derrida, *Margins of Philosphy*, trans. Alan Bass (Chicago, 1982) p.27.
6. David Jenkins, 'Literature and the Theologian' in John Coulson (ed.), *Theology and the University* (Baltimore and London, 1964) p.219.
7. David H. Hesla, 'Religion and Literature: the Second Stage', *Journal of the American Academy of Relgion*, XLVI/2, 181.
8. See, Meir Sternberg, *The Poetics of Biblical Narrative* (Bloomington, 1985) pp.7ff.
9. John Coulson, *Religion and Imagination, 'in aid of a grammar of assent'* (Oxford, 1981) p.3.
10. See, Robert Detweiler (ed.), *Art/Literature/Religion: Life on the Borders. Journal of the American Academy of Religion Thematic Studies*, 49/2 (Chicago, 1983) p.1.
11. Ziolkowski, 'Literature and the Bible: a Comparatist's Appeal' in Detweiler, op. cit., p.185.
12. See, Jasper, *Coleridge as Poet and Religious Thinker* (London, 1985), 'The Role of the Poet', pp.11–13.
13. Stopford A. Brooke, *Theology in the English Poets*, 2nd edn (London, 1874) p.2.
14. T. S. Eliot, *Selected Essays*, 3rd edn (London, 1951) p.388.
15. He later revised his opinion of Herbert, and came to regard him as a major poet. See op. cit., p.391.
16. John J. McDonald in 'Religion and Literature' (*Religion and Literature*, 16.1, 1984, 61–71) would disagree with this understanding of Eliot's essay. He sees Eliot reducing literature to a supplementary role to religion, while Eliot's respect for the independence of literature 'has an air of nostalgia about it'.

CHAPTER 2: POETRY, BELIEF AND DEVOTION

1. Boswell, *Life of Johnson*, (Oxford, 1953; 3rd edn 1799) p.1293.
2. Ibid., p.1781.
3. Samuel Johnson, *Lives of the Poets*, 2 vols (Oxford, 1952; 1st edn 1781) I. pp.202–4.
4. See, Laurence Lerner, 'Religious Poetry: Alive and Well?', *Theology*, LXXXIII, 1980, 354–9.
5. W. B. Yeats, Preface to *The Ten Principal Upanishads* (with Shri Purohit Swami), London, 1937) p.10.
6. See further, Cleanth Brooks, 'Religion and Literature', *Sewannee Review*, 82, 1974, 101–2.
7. Quoted in Charles Gordon Clark, 'Christianity in Kipling's Verse', *Theology*, LXXXV, 1982, 36–7.
8. T. S. Eliot 'The Humanism of Irving Babbitt' (1928), *Selected Essays*, 3rd edn (London, 1951) p.475.
9. R. S. Thomas, Introduction to *A Choice of George Herbert's Verse* (London, 1967) p.16.
10. See, Dom Illtyd Trethowan, 'Natural Theology and its relation to poetry' in John Coulson (ed.), *Theology and the University*, (Baltimore and London, 1964) p.207.
11. A. M. Allchin, *The World Is a Wedding* (London, 1978) p. 132.
12. Helen Gardner, *Religion and Literature* (London, 1971) p.142.
13. Auden, *Collected Longer Poems* (London, 1974) p.171.
14. Auden, *The Dyer's Hand and Other Essays* (London 1963) p.57.
15. John Wesley, quoted in Geoffrey Wainwright, *Doxology: a Systematic Theology* (London 1980) p.202.
16. Johnson, *Lives of the Poets*, II, p.367. '[Watts')/ devotional poetry is, like that of others, unsatisfactory. The paucity of its topics enforces perpetual repetition, and the sanctity of the matter rejects the ornaments of figurative diction'.
17. Isaac Watts, quoted in Donald Davie, *A Gathered Church: the Literature of the English Dissenting Interest, 1700–1930* (London and Henley, 1978) p.24.
18. John Keble 'Sacred Poetry' (1825) in, Edmund D. Jones (ed.), *Nineteenth Century English Critical Essays* (Oxford, 1947) p. 173.
19. D. H. Lawrence, 'Hymns in a Man's Life' (1928) in Anthony Beal (ed.), *Selected Literary Criticsm* (London, 1956) p.9.
20. See further, J. R. Watson, 'The Victorian Hymn', an Inaugural Lecture, Durham University (1981) pp.12–13.
21. Wainwright, op. cit., pp.205–10.
22. H. E. W. Turner, 'Communicatio Idiomatum' in Alan Richardson and John Bowden (eds), *A New Dictionary of Christian Theology* (London, 1983) p.113.
23. J. H. Newman, 'Poetry with reference to Aristotle's Poetics' (1829) in Edmund D. Jones (ed.), *Nineteenth Century English Critical Essays*, (Oxford, 1947) p.212.
24. Farrer, 'Poetic Truth' *Reflective Faith*, ed. Charles C. Conti (London, 1972) p.37.

25. Helen Gardner's wish to safeguard as normative the 'main' or 'literal' sense of great literature, is dangerously close to defining *all* literature as of second order language and thus descending into dogmatism and literalism. See *In Defence of the Imagination* (Oxford, 1982), esp. ch. V.

26. David Jones, Preface to *The Anathemata: Fragments of an Attempted Writing*, 2nd edn (London and Boston, 1972) p.33.

27. Throughout this discussion, reference is made to John Tinsley, 'Tell it Slant', *Theology*, LXXXIII, 1980, 163, 70.

28. Søren Kierkegaard, *The Point of View for My Work as an Author*, quoted in Tinsley, op. cit., p.167.

29. See, Farrer, *Interpretation and Belief*, ed. Charles C. Conti (London, 1976) pp.39–53.

30. See, John Crowe Ransom, 'Poetry: a Note in Ontology', in James Scully (ed.), *Modern Poets on Modern Poetry*, (Fontana, 1966) pp.102–3.

31. See further, Nathan A. Scott Jr, *The Poetics of Belief* (Chapel Hill and London, 1985) pp.45–6.

CHAPTER 3: THE POETRY OF THE RESURRECTION

1. H. Conzelmann, quoted in W. Pannenberg, *Jesus – God and Man* (London, 1968) p.98. Pannenberg criticizes this position, asserting that the argument from presuppositions concerning general laws of nature does not necessarily impose definitive judgements upon the possibility or impossibility of an individual event.

2. See, Nicholas Lash, 'Easter Meaning', *The Heythrop Journal*, XXV, 1984, 7.

3. Iris Murdoch, quoted in A. S. Byatt, *Iris Murdoch* (The British Council, 1976) p.15; D. H. Lawrence, *Selected Literary Criticism*, ed. Anthony Beal (London, 1967) p.105. S. T. Coleridge, *Biographia Literaria: The Collected Works*, 7, eds James Engell and W. Jackson Bate (Princeton, 1983) I, p.9.

4. Rowan Williams, *Resurrection* (London, 1982) p.91.

5. Op. cit., p.110.

6. See, M. R. James, *The Apocryphal New Testament* (Oxford, 1924) p.90.

7. See Pannenberg, op. cit., p.104.

8. Coleridge, *Confessions of an Inquiring Spirit*, ed. Henry Nelson Coleridge (London, 1840) p.13. ' . . . in the Bible there is more that *finds* me than I have experienced in all other books put together'.

9. See, A. M. Ramsey, *The Resurrection of Christ* (Fontana, 1961) p.39. 'It is by their readiness to welcome such inquiry and to participate in it that the teachers of Christianity make good their claim that the Gospel rests upon fact.'

10. Op. cit., p.9.

CHAPTER 4: MORALITY AND THE TEXT

1. Pound, *Letters 1907–1941*, ed. D. D. Paige (London, 1951) p.248. See also, Martin Jarrett-Kerr, 'Literature and Commitment: "Choosing Sides" ' in David Jasper (ed.), *Images of Belief in Literature*, (London, 1984) pp.105–6.
2. Eliot, 'The *Pensées* of Pascal' in *Selected Essays*, 3rd edn (London, 1951) pp.402–16.
3. J. H. Newman, *An Essay in Aid of a Grammar of Assent* (1870). See. John Coulson, *Religion and Imagination 'in aid of a grammar of assent'* (Oxford, 1981) pp.130–1.
4. Terence Hawkes, *Structuralism and Semiotics* (London, 1977) p.153.
5. Roland Barthes, *Sur Racine* (Paris, 1963) pp.171–2.
6. W. K. Wimsatt Jr and Monroe C. Beardsley, 'The Intentional Fallacy' in *The Verbal Icon. Studies in the Meaning of Poetry* (Lexington, Ky, 1954) p.5.
7. Eliot, *Selected Essays*, p.388.
8. See, Wayne C. Booth, *The Rhetoric of Fiction* (Chicago, 1961) p.377.
9. S. T. Coleridge, *Biographia Literaria* (1817), eds James Engell and W. Jackson Bate (Princeton, 1983), I, p.303.
10. Alasdair Macintyre, *After Virtue* (London, 1981) p.223.
11. Stanley Hauerwas, 'Constancy and Forgiveness: the Novel as a School For Virtue', *Notre Dame English Journal*, XV, 3, 1983, 43.
12. David Lodge, Introduction to the Penguin Edition (1985) p.7.
13. See, for example, Horton Davies, *Catching the Conscience: Essays in Religion and Literature* (Cambridge, Mass. 1984) ch.7.
14. See more generally, Wayne C. Booth, op. cit. p.382.
15. See, Wesley A. Kort, *Moral Fiber, Character and Belief in Recent American Fiction* (Philadelphia, 1982) p.6.
16. See also below, chapter 6, p.94, and the discussion of Paul Ricoeur on metaphor.
17. Hauerwas, op. cit., p.47.

CHAPTER 5: BEAUTY, THE TRUE AND THE GOOD

1. See also, George Steiner, *Real Presences*, The Leslie Stephen Memorial Lecture, 1985 (Cambridge, 1986) pp.14–16.
2. Hans Urs von Balthasar, *The Glory of the Lord: a Theological Aesthetics I: Seeing the Form*, trans. Erasmo Leiva-Merikakis (Edinburgh, 1982) p.18.
3. Ogden and Richards, *The Meaning of Meanings*, 10th edn, (London, 1949) p.139.
4. Lukács, *The Theory of the Novel* (1920) trans. Anna Bostock (London, 1971) p.16.
5. David Simpson (ed.), *German Aesthetic and Literary Criticism: Kant, Fichte, Schelling, Schopenhauer, Hegel* (Cambridge, 1984) p.2.
6. Kant, *The Critique of Judgement*, trans. James Creed Meredith, (Oxford, 1952) p.51.

7. See further, Hans Robert Jauss, *Toward an Aesthetic of Reception*, trans. Timothy Bahti (Brighton, 1982) p.80.
8. Scruton, *Kant* (Oxford, 1982) p.87.
9. See further, Hilary Fraser, *Beauty and Belief: Aesthetics and Religion in Victorian Literature* (Cambridge, 1986) pp.136–82.
10. See, Mary Warnock, 'Imagination – Aesthetic and Religious', *Theology* LXXXIII, 1980, 403–9.
11. See Gordon D. Kaufman, *The Theological Imagination. Constructing the Concept of God* (Philadelphia, 1981) p.23.
12. Warnock, op. cit., p.409.
13. See Giles Gunn, *the Interpretation of Otherness* (New York, 1979) pp.58–60.
14. Ricoeur, *Time and Narrative*, vol. 1, trans, Kathleen McLaughlin and David Pellauer (Chicago and London, 1984) p.64.
15. Stephen Sykes, 'The Role of Story in the Christian Religion: a Suggestion', *Literature and Theology*, vol.I. i, 1987, 19–20.
16. Jauss, op. cit., p.4.
17. See my *The New Testament and the Literary Imagination* (London, 1987) p.20–1.
18. I am not prepared to accept the sad negatives of Professor Frank Kermode in the conclusion of his excellent book *The Genesis of Secrecy* (Harvard, 1979). 'World and book, it may be, are hopelessly plural, endlessly disappointing; we stand alone before them, aware of their arbitrariness and impenetrability . . . our sole hope and pleasure is in the perception of a momentary radiance before the door of disappointment is finally shut on us.' (p.145). The form of the text sustains, it seems to me, a deeper assurance than Kermode is prepared to admit.
19. Frank Burch Brown, *Transfiguration. Poetic Metaphor and the Languages of Religious Belief* (Chapel Hill and London, 1983) p.8.
20. See also, Margarita Stocker, 'God in Theory: Literature and Theodicy', *Literature and Theology*, vol. I. i, 1987, 70–88.
21. See further, Leiva-Merikakis, 'Of Ecstasy and Judgement: Three Moments in the Approach to Beauty' in Robert Detweiler (ed.), *Art/Literature/Religion: Life on the Borders*, p.94.
22. Robert Alter, *The Art of Biblical Poetry*, (New York, 1985) p.9.
23. Shklovsky, 'Art as Technique' in L. T. Leman and M. J. Reis (eds), *Russian Formalist Criticism* (Lincoln, Nebr., 1965) p.21.
24. J. G. Herder oberved this in 1782 in *Von Geist der erbräischer Poesie.*
25. For a detailed, and neglected, analysis, see Austin Farrer, *A Study in St. Mark* (Westminster, 1951).
26. Steiner, op. cit., p.19.

CHAPTER 6: HERMENEUTICS, LITERARY THEORY AND THE BIBLE

1. Geoffrey H. Hartman 'The Struggle for the Text' in Hartman and Sanford Budick (eds), *Midrash and Literature* (Yale, 1986) p.3.

2. Johnson, *Lives of the Poet* (1781) 2 vols (Oxford, 1952) 'The Life of Milton', I, p.127.
3. I am grateful to Margarita Stocker for drawing my attention to these poems in this context.
4. Enright, 'The History of World Languages' in *Collected Poems, 1987* (Oxford, 1987) p.206.
5. English translation by Wade Baskin, *Course in General Linguistics* (London, 1960).
6. Terence Hawkes, *Structuralism and Semiotics*, p.20.
7. See also, Jonathan Culler, *Saussure*, (Fontana, 1976) p.23.
8. See Hawkes, op. cit., p.152.
9. See also, Paul de Man, *Blindness and Insight. Essays in the Rhetoric of Contemporary Criticism*, 2nd edn (Minneapolis, 1983) p.233.
10. See Lynn M. Poland, *Literary criticism and Biblical Hermeneutics: a Critique of Formalist approaches*, AAR Academy Series 48 (Chico, 1985) p.193.
11. Margarita Stocker, *Apocalyptic Marvell: the Second Coming in Seventeenth Century Poetry* (Brighton, 1986) pp.105–13.
12. Friedrich Schleiermacher, *Hermeneutics: the Handwritten Manuscripts*, trans. James Duke and Jack Forstman, AAR Texts and Translations Series, 1, (Missoula, 1977) p.150.
13. Rudolf Bultmann, 'New Testament and Mythology' in *Kerygma and Myth*, ed Hans Werner Bartsch, trans R. H. Fuller (New York, 1961), I, p.10.
14. See further Susanne K. Langer, *Philosophy in a New Key* (New York, 1951).
15. David E. Klemm, *The Hermeneutical Theory of Paul Ricoeur* (London and Toronto, 1983) p.11.
16. Don Cupitt, *Taking Leave of God* (London, 1980) pp.67, 45.
17. See Janet Martin Soskice, *Metaphor and Religious Language* (Oxford, 1985) pp.142–3.
18. Ian T. Ramsey, *Models for Divine Activity*, (London, 1973) p.58.

CHAPTER 7: THE LIMITS OF FORMALISM AND THE THEOLOGY OF HOPE

1. George Steiner, *Tolstoy or Dostoyevsky*, rev. edn (Harmondsworth, 1967) pp. 11–14.
2. See E. D. Hirsch Jr, *Validity in Interpretation* (New Haven and London, 1967) pp. 19–23, 51–7.
3. Paul Ricoeur, *Time and Narrative*, vol. I, trans. McLaughlin and Pellauer (Chicago and London, 1984) pp. 47– 8.
4. Contra, David Hesla, 'Religion and Literature: the Second Stage', *Journal of the American Academy of Religion*, XLVI/2, 181.
5. Ricoeur, *The Symbolism of Evil*, trans. Emerson Buchanan (Boston, 1967) p. 351, ' . . . if we can no longer live the great symbolisms of the sacred in accordance with the original belief in them, we can, we modern men, aim at a second naïveté in and through criticism'.

6. In Ricoeur, *Hermeneutics and the Human Sciences* (Cambridge and Paris, 1981) pp. 131–44.
7. George A. Lindbeck, *The Nature of Doctrine, Religion and Theology in a Post-liberal Age* (London, 1984) p. 38.
8. Ricoeur, 'Freedom in the Light of Hope' in *Essays in Biblical Interpretation*, ed. Lewis S. Mudge (London, 1981) p. 159.
9. de Man, *Blindness and Insight*, pp. 229–45.
10. Empson, *Seven Types of Ambiguity* (London, 1984) p. 192.
11. In, Moltmann, *The Experiment Hope* (London, 1975) pp. 85–100.
12. J. Hillis Miller, *The Form of Victorian Fiction* (Notre Dame and London, 1968) p. 36.
13. I have drawn the phrases which follow from the abbreviated version of Steiner's lecture, published in the *Times Literary Supplement*, 8 Nov. 1985, 1262–76.

CHAPTER 8: BEYOND FORMALISM

1. *Roland Barthes by Roland Barthes* (1975), trans. Richard Howard, in Susan Sontag, *Barthes: Selected Writings* (Fontana, 1983) pp. 418–19.
2. See, Christopher Norris, *Deconstruction: Theory and Practice* (London and New York, 1082) p. 4.
3. Coleridge, *Lay Sermons*, ed. R. J. White, *The Collected Works*, 6, (Princeton, 1972), p. 30. For a general discussion see Stephen Prickett, *Romanticisim and Religion: the Tradition of Coleridge and Wordsworth in the Victorian Church* (Cambridge, 1976).
4. See further, Dominic Baker-Smith, 'Exegesis: Literary and Divine', in David Jasper (ed.), *Images of Belief in Literature*, pp. 169–78.
5. Jameson, *The Prison-House of Language: a Critical Account of Structuralism and Russian Formalism* (Princeton, 1972) pp. 5–6.
6. See, Hawkes, *Structuralism and Semiotics*, p. 19.
7. Derrida, *Of Grammatology* (1967), trans. Gayatri Chakrovorty Spivak. (Baltimore and London, 1976) p. 6.
8. For an account of this context see Mark C. Taylor, 'Introduction: System . . . Structure . . . Difference . . . Other' in Taylor (ed.), *Deconstruction in Context*, pp. 1–34.
9. See further, Robert Detweiler, *Story, Sign, and Self. Phenomenology and Structuralism as Literary-Critical Methods* (Philadelphia, 1978) p. 20.
10. George Gordon, quoted in Terry Eagleton, *Literary Theory*, p. 23.
11. J. Hillis Miller, *The Disappearance of God: Five 19th-Century Writers* (Harvard, 1963).
12. See, Ray L. Hart, *Unfinished Man and the Imagination: Toward an Ontology and a Rhetoric of Revelation*, repr. (Atlanta, 1985) pp. 37ff.
13. Thomas J. J. Altizer and William Hamilton, *Radical Theology and the Death of God* (Harmondsworth, 1968) pp. 170–1.
14. Cupitt, *Taking Leave of God*, p. 139.

CHAPTER 9: THEODICY AND DECONSTRUCTION

1. See further, Ray L. Hart, *Unfinished Man and the Imagination*, p. 38.
2. Christopher Norris, *Deconstruction: Theory and Practice*, p. 19.
3. Eagleton, *Literary Theory*, p. 147.
4. Jacques Derrida, *Of Grammatology*, p. 43.
5. Norris, op. cit., p. 49.
6. Austin Farrer, *Love Almighty and Ills Unlimited* (Fontana, 1966) p. 62.
7. See, Farrer, 'The Prior Actuality of God' (1966) repr. in *Reflective Faith*, pp. 179–80.
8. See. John Hick, *Evil and the God of Love* (Fontana, 1968) pp. 160–66.
9. Leibniz, *Theodicy*, trans. E. M. Huggard, ed. Farrer (London, 1951) para. 225.
10. Farrer, Introduction to *Theodicy*, pp. 9–10.
11. Quoted in, John Butt, Introduction to *Candide* (Harmondsworth, 1947) p. 9.
12. See further, A. L. Loades, *Kant and Job's Comforters* (Newcastle, 1985) p. 87.
13. See, Frank Kermode, *The Genesis of Secrecy: on the Interpretation of Narrative* (Cambridge, Mass. and London, 1979) pp. 125–45.
14. Farrer, *Faith and Speculation* (London, 1967) p. 76.
15. Kant, *Prolegomena to Any Future Metaphysics That Will Be Able To Present Itself as a Science*, trans, P. G. Lucas (Manchester, 1966) p. 124.
16. See, Dominic Baker-Smith 'Exegesis: Literary and Divine', p. 171.
17. See, Eagleton, op. cit., pp. 133–4.
18. Fish, *Surprised by Sin: the Reader in Paradise Lost* (London and New York, 1967) p. 5.
19. Ray L. Hart, op. cit., p. 38.
20. Compare S. T. Coleridge's familiar words from ch. 13 of *Biographia Literaria*: 'The primary IMAGINATION I hold to be the living Power and prime Agent of all human Perception, and as a repetition in the finite mind of the eternal act of creation in the infinite I AM.'
21. William F. Lynch, *Christ and Apollo: the Dimensions of the Literary Imagination* (Notre Dame, 1975) p. 161.
22. Farrer, *A Celebration of Faith*, ed. L. Houlden (London, 1972) p. 122.
23. Frank Kermode in his paper, 'The Uses of Error' (*Theology*, LXXXIX, 1986, 425–31) discusses De La Tour's painting at length, with the debate over the figure of Job's wife, as compassionate – or scolding. Her expression is as ambiguous as her sentence, 'Curse God and die', a translation of the Hebrew euphemistic 'bless'?
24. See also, Stephen Prickett, 'Towards a Rediscovery of the Bible. The Problem of the Still Small Voice,' in Michael Wadsworth (ed.), *Ways of Reading the Bible* (Brighton, 1981) pp. 105–17.
25. See also, Horace H. Underwood, 'Derrida and the Christian Critics: a Response to Clarence Walhout,' *Christianity and Literature*, XXXV, Spring 1986, 7–12.

CONCLUSION

1. Cleanth Brooks, 'Religion and Literature,' *Sewanee Review*, 82, 1974, 103, 106.
2. William Wordsworth, 'Essay, Supplementary to the Preface to "Lyrical Ballads", 1815', *Poetical Works*, eds Thomas Hutchinson and Revd Ernest de Selincourt (Oxford, 1969) p. 744.
3. David Hesla, 'Religion and Literature: the Second Stage', *Journal of the American Academy of Religion*, XLVI/2, 189.
4. John J. McDonald, 'Religion and Literature', *Religion and Literature* (Formerly *The Notre Dame English Journal*), 16. 1, 1984, 65.

Bibliography

(This is a selected number of critical works which have been particularly important in the writing of this book.)
There are three journals directly concerned with religion and literature.

Religion and Literature (Notre Dame)
Christianity and Literature (Waco, Texas)
Literature and Theology (Oxford)

Robert Alter, *The Art of Biblical Narrative* (London, 1981)
——, *The Art of Biblical Poetry* (New York, 1985).
Hans Urs von Balthasar, *The Glory of the Lord: a Theological Aesthetics*, I: Seeing the Form, trans. Erasmo Leiva-Merikakis (Edinburgh, 1982).
J. A. W. Bennett, *Poetry of the Passion Studies in Twelve Centuries of English Verse* (Oxford 1982).
Cleanth Brook, 'Religion and Literature', *Sewanee Review*, 82, 1974, 93–107.
Frank Burch Brown, *Transfiguration: Poetic Metaphor and the Languages of Religious Belief* (Chapel Hill and London, 1983).
John Coulson, *Religion and Imagination 'in aid of a grammar of assent'*, (Oxford, 1981).
David Daiches, *God and the Poets* (Oxford, 1984).
Jacques Derrida, *Of Grammatology*, trans. Gayatri Chakravorty Spivak (Baltimore and London, 1976).
Robert Detweiler, *Story, Sign, and Self: Phenomenology and Structuralism as Literary-Critical Methods* (Philadelphia, 1978).
——, ed. *Art/Literature/Religion: Life on the Borders, Journal of the American Academy of Religion Studies*, vol. XLIX, no. 2 (Chico, 1983) (Contains a useful bibliography, mainly of American works).
Terry Eagleton, *Literary Theory: an Introduction* (Oxford, 1983).
Michael Edwards, *Towards a Christian Poetics* (London, 1984).
T. S. Eliot, *Selected Essays*, 3rd edn. (London, 1951).
Austin Farrer, *The Glass of Vision* (Westminster, 1948).
——, 'Poetic Truth' in *Reflective Faith*, ed. Charles C. Conti (London, 1972) pp. 24–38.
Northrop Frye, *The Great Code: The Bible and Literature* (London, 1982).
Helen Gardner, *Religion and Literature* (London, 1971).
——, *In Defence of the Imagination* (Oxford, 1982).
Giles Gunn, *The Interpretation of Otherness: Literature, Religion, and the American Imagination* (New York, 1979).

Ray L. Hart, *Unfinished Man and the Imagination: Toward an Ontology and a Rhetoric of Revelation* (Atlanta, 1985).

Geoffrey H. Hartman and Sanford Budick (eds), *Midrash and Literature* (New Haven and London, 1986).

Terence Hawkes, *Structuralism and Semiotics* (London, 1977).

David Hesla, 'Religion and Literature: the Second Stage'. *Journal of the American Academy of Religion*, XLVI/2, 181–92.

David Jasper (ed.), *Images of Belief in Literature* (London, 1984).

——, *The Interpretation of Belief: Coleridge, Schleiermacher and Romanticism* (London, 1986).

——, *The New Testament and the Literary Imagination* (London, 1987).

John Keble, 'Sacred Poetry' (1825) in Edmund D. Jones (ed.), *Nineteenth Century English Critical Essays* (Oxford, 1947) pp. 162–89.

Frank Kermode, *The Genesis of Secrecy: on the Interpretation of Narrative* (Harvard, 1979).

Wesley A. Kort, *Modern Fiction and Human Time: a Study in Narrative and Belief* (Tampa, 1985).

William F. and Lynch, S. J., *Christ and Apollo: the Dimensions of the Literary Imagination* (Notre Dame, 1975).

Laurence Lerner, 'Religious Poetry: Alive and Well?', *Theology*, LXXXIII, 1980, 354–9.

John J. McDonald, 'Religion and Literature', *Religion and Literature*, 16, 1984, 61–71.

Paul de Man, *Blindness and Insight: Essays in the Rhetoric of Contemporary Criticism*, 2nd edn (Minneapolis, 1983).

J. H. Newman, 'Poetry with reference to Aristotle's Poetics' (1829) in Edmund D. Jones (ed.), *Nineteenth Century English Critical Essays* (Oxford, 1947) pp. 190– 215.

Christopher Norris, *Deconstruction: Theory and Practice* (London, 1982).

Lynn M. Poland, *Literary Criticism and Biblical Hermeneutics: a Critique of Formalist Approaches*, AAR Academy Series 48 (Chico, 1985).

Paul Ricouer, 'Biblical Hermeneutics', *Semeia*, 4 (1975), ed. J. D. Crossan.

——, *The Rule of Metaphor: Multi-Disciplinary Studies of the Creation of Meaning in Language*, trans. Robert Czerny (Toronto, 1977).

——, *Time and Narrative*, vol. I, trans. Kathleen McLaughlin and David Pellauer (Chicago, 1984).

Ferdinand de Saussure, *Course in General Linguistics*, trans. Wade Baskin (London, 1960).

Nathan A. Scott, Jr, *The Poetics of Belief. Studies in Coleridge, Arnold, Pater, Sautayana, Stevens and Heidegger* (Chapel Hill and London, 1985). (Nathan Scott has written numerous books on religion and literature. Important also are *The Broken Center* (1966), *Craters of the Spirit* (1968), *Negative Capability* (1969), *The Wild Prayer of Longing* (1971).

Janet Martin Soskice, *Metaphor and Religious Language* (Oxford, 1985).

George Steiner, *Real Presences*, The Leslie Stephen Memorial Lecture, 1985 (Cambridge, 1986).

Meir Sternberg, *The Poetics of Biblical Narrative* (Bloomington, 1985).

Margarita Stocker, 'God in Theory: Milton, Literature and Theodicy', *Literature and Theodicy*, 1 (1987) 70–88.

John Tinsley, 'Tell it Slant', *Theology*, LXXXIII, 1983, 163–70.
Michael Wadsworth (ed.), *Ways of Reading the Bible*. (Brighton, 1981). (Particularly valuable is Stephen Prickett's essay, 'Towards a Rediscovery of the Bible: the Problem of the Still Small Voice', expanded in his more recent book *Words and 'The Word'* [Cambridge, 1986]).
W. K. Wimsatt Jr and Monroe C. Beardsley, 'The Intentional Fallacy', repr. in *The Verbal Icon. Studies in the Meaning of Poetry* (Lexington, Ky, 1984) pp. 3–39.
T. R. Wright, *Theology and Literature* (Oxford, 1988).
Theodore Ziolkowski, *Fictional Transfigurations of Jesus* (Princeton, 1972).

Index